Elementary Poetry

Textbook and Activity Book

by Sonja Glumich

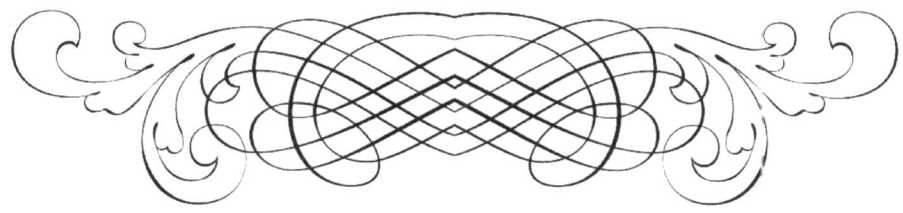

Poetry Study for Elementary School-Aged Children

Volume 2: Poetry of Fables, Fairies, and Fauna

Interweaves poetry, vocabulary, mapwork, discussion, copywork, narration, and dictation

Under the Home Press Division
www.underthehome.org

Front Cover
Take the Fair Face of Woman, and Gently Suspending, With Butterflies, Flowers, and Jewels
Attending, Thus Your Fairy is Made of Most Beautiful Things
Painting by Sophie Gengembre Anderson
License: The author died in 1903, so this work is in the public domain in its country of origin and other countries and areas where the copyright term is the author's life plus 100 years or less. This work is in the public domain in the United States because it was published (or registered with the U.S. Copyright Office) before January 1, 1925.
original source: commons.wikimedia.org/wiki/File:SophieAndersonTakethefairfaceofWoman.jpg

Copyright © 2020 Sonja Glumich
All rights reserved.

No part of this work may be reproduced, scanned, or electronically transmitted without prior permission of the copyright owner unless actions are expressly permitted by federal law the family exception detailed below.

The copyright owner grants an exception for photocopying or scanning and printing pages for use within an immediate family or homeschool co-op only. Scanned pages should never be used for any other purpose including sharing between families, posting online, transmitting electronically, or resale.

This exception does not extend to schools, however a reasonable licensing fee for reproduction can be negotiated by contacting Under the Home, the publisher.

For more information or to report errata, please contact Under the Home at contact@underthehome.org.

ISBN-13: 978-1948783040

DEDICATION

For Chris, Everett, Cassidy, and Calista – my beloved family and curricula test squad.

TABLE OF CONTENTS

PART I: POETRY OF FABLES BY JEAN DE LA FONTAINE

Lesson 1. The Frog Who Wished to be as Big as the Ox 1
Lesson 2. The Grasshopper and the Ant 4
Lesson 3. The Cat and the Fox 7
Lesson 4. The Dog and His Image 11
Lesson 5. The Raven and the Fox 14
Lesson 6. The City Mouse and the Country Mouse 17
Lesson 7. The Dove and the Ant 20
Lesson 8. The Fox and the Grapes 23
Lesson 9. The Fox and the Stork 26
Lesson 10. The Hare and the Tortoise 30
Lesson 11. The Heron Who Was Hard to Please 34
Lesson 12. The Lion and the Gnat 38

PART II: POETRY OF FAIRIES BY WILLIAM ALLINGHAM

Lesson 13. The Fairies 42
Lesson 14. The Elf Singing 46
Lesson 15. The Fairy King 50
Lesson 16. Chorus of Fairies 54
Lesson 17. The Fairy Shoemaker 58

PART III: POETRY OF FAUNA BY VARIOUS

Lesson 18. Robin Redbreast 62
Lesson 19. Dreaming 65
Lesson 20. I Love You, Dear 68
Lesson 21. Seasons 71
Lesson 22. The Cat and the Dog 74
Lesson 23. The Bird 78
Lesson 24. Wishing 82
Lesson 25. I Saw a Little Birdie Fly 85
Lesson 26. A Mountain Round 88
Lesson 27. Birds' Names 91
Lesson 28. Nick Spence 94
Lesson 29. Riding 97
Lesson 30. Tom Cricket 101
Lesson 31. Let Dogs Delight to Bark and Bite 105
Lesson 32. The Owl & the Pussy Cat 108
Lesson 33. A Chrysalis 112
Lesson 34. The Raven v. 1-6 116
Lesson 35. The Raven v. 7-12 121
Lesson 36. The Raven v. 13-18 126

ANSWERS TO REVIEW QUESTIONS 132
REFERENCES AND ADDITIONAL READING 138

Goals of This Book Series

This book series aims to familiarize children with works of poetry from an early age, nurture the imagination, inspire an appreciation for beauty, encourage a mind for symbolism and nuance, foster the ability to narrate and dictate complex ideas, and expand children's vocabularies. Lessons are short and interactive by design to target elementary school-aged children.

Inspiration for This Book Series

Charlotte Mason, born in 1842, sought to provide teaching advice and strategies to instructors and homeschooling parents. She detailed her educational philosophies and methodologies in her multi-volume *Home Education Series*. She advocated for centering instruction around living works, such as the finest art, music, poetry, and prose. Mason recommended that from an early age, children engage in the regular study of poetry, including reciting poetry. In her *Home Education Series*, she writes, "…include a good deal of poetry, to accustom him to the delicate rendering of shades of meaning, and especially to make him aware that words are beautiful in themselves, that they are a source of pleasure, and are worthy of our honour; and that a beautiful word deserves to be beautifully said, with a certain roundness of tone and precision of utterance."

The Targeted Audience for This Book

This book targets elementary school-aged children in grades one and up.

Overview of This Book

This book provides 36 lessons or enough for one lesson per week over a standard 36-week school year. This volume highlights poems of fables, fairies, and fauna from the fabulist Jean de La Fontaine, William Allingham, Edward Lear, Edgar Allan Poe, and additional master poets. The selected poems in this book appeal to children and their adult instructors by featuring impish fairies, mischievous animals, and fables of moral lessons.

How to Teach Using This Book

The table below outlines the recommended instructional approach to teach a 36-week course using this book.

Every Week – Introduce a New Poem	
Section Title	**Section Instructions**
Featured Poem	• Students study one poem per week over the 36-week school year. • Students recite the poem line by line with instructor assistance.
Synopsis	Instructors read the synopsis of the poem to students.
Recite Poem Information	Students practice reciting the poem title and the name of the poet.
Narrate the Poem	Students verbally summarize the poem in their own words.
Study Poem Pictures	Students describe how the included pictures relate to the poem.
Can You Find It?	Students find and point out items in the poem pictures.
Act Out the Poem	Students act out aspects of the poem.
Explore Rhyming	Instructors help students find and recite rhyming words in poems.
Vocabulary	• Students practice pronouncing the featured vocabulary words. • Instructors read the definitions of vocabulary words to the students.
Answer Review Questions	• Instructors ask students the review questions. • The end of the book contains answers to review questions.
Trace or Copy the Excerpt	Students trace and/or copy the provided poem excerpt.
Draw the Poem	Students create novel artwork based on the poem.

PART I: POETRY OF FABLES

LESSON 1: "THE FROG WHO WISHED TO BE AS BIG AS THE OX" BY JEAN DE LA FONTAINE

FEATURED POEM

There was a little Frog

Whose home was in a bog,

And he worried 'cause he wasn't big enough.

He sees an ox and cries:

"That's just about my size,

If I stretch myself–Say Sister, see me puff!"

So he blew, blew, blew,

Saying: "Sister, will that do?"

But she shook her head. And then he lost his wits.

For he stretched and puffed again

Till he cracked beneath the strain,

And burst, and flew about in little bits.

SYNOPSIS

A frog wishes for the impossible, to be as big as an ox. When he puffs up to grow bigger, he bursts into little bits.

ENRICHMENT ACTIVITIES

1. **Recite Poem Information**
   Practice reciting the title of the poem and the name of the poet.
2. **Narrate the Poem**
   Verbally recount poem events in your own words.
3. **Study the Poem Picture**
   Study the poem picture and describe how it relates to the poem.
4. **Can You Find It?**
   Find the following in the poem picture: Puffed up frog, smaller frogs, grass, and bog.

5. **Act Out the Poem**
    - Pretend to be the little frog puffing up to be an ox.
    - Puff out your cheeks and try to make yourself as big as possible.
    - Can you make yourself as big as an ox?

6. **Discuss the Poem**
    - In the poem, the frog tries to be something that he isn't.
    - Have you ever wished to be someone else? Why?
    - Discuss why it is wonderful to be you.

7. **Explore Rhyming**
    - Many poems have lines ending in words that rhyme.
    - Words that rhyme share similar ending sounds.
    - Rhyming word pairs in the lesson poem include frog and bog, cries and size, and wits and bits.
    - Find and recite the rhyming words in the poem.

VOCABULARY

Students Recite Words	Students Listen to the Definitions
bog	A marsh or swamp.
ox	An adult male of cattle.
blew	Produced an air current from the mouth.
wits	The ability to think rationally and using common sense.
cracked	To break apart under pressure.
burst	To break from internal pressure.

REVIEW QUESTIONS

1. What is the title of the poem?
2. What happens in the poem?
3. What is the setting of the poem?
4. Who are the characters in the poem?
5. What does the poem teach the reader?

TRACEWORK AND/OR COPYWORK

Say Sister, see me puff!

DRAW THE POEM (Depict a swamp and the plants and animals within it.)

ELEMENTARY POETRY VOLUME 2: POETRY OF FABLES, FAIRIES, AND FAUNA

LESSON 2: "THE GRASSHOPPER AND THE ANT" BY JEAN DE LA FONTAINE

FEATURED POEM

The Grasshopper, singing
All summer long,
Now found winter stinging,
And ceased in his song.
Not a morsel or crumb in his cupboard-
So he shivered, and ceased in his song.

Miss Ant was his neighbor;
To her he went:
"O, you're rich from labor,
And I've not a cent.
Lend me food, and I vow I'll return it,
Though at present I have not a cent."

The Ant's not a lender,
I must confess.
Her heart's far from tender
To one in distress.
So she said: "Pray, how passed you the summer,
That in winter you come to distress?"

"I sang through the summer,"
Grasshopper said.
"But now I am glummer
Because I've no bread."
"So you sang!" sneered the Ant. "That relieves me.
Now it's winter-go dance for your bread!"

SYNOPSIS

A grasshopper sings all summer instead of saving food for winter and grows hungry. A hardworking ant who stockpiled food all summer long refuses to share with the grasshopper.

ENRICHMENT ACTIVITIES

1. **Recite Poem Information**
   Practice reciting the title of the poem and the name of the poet.
2. **Narrate the Poem**
   Verbally recount poem events in your own words.
3. **Study the Poem Picture**
   Study the poem picture and describe how it relates to the poem.
4. **Can You Find It?**
   Find the following in the poem picture: Grasshopper, ants, violin, and grain.
5. **Act Out the Poem**
   - Pretend to be the grasshopper and sing away your summer days.
   - Act like the hardworking ant, spending your summer storing food for winter.
6. **Discuss the Poem**
   - Explore why you think the grasshopper failed to save food for winter.
   - Discuss whether or not you think the ant should have shared with the grasshopper.
7. **Explore Rhyming**
   Find and recite the rhyming words in the poem.

VOCABULARY

Students Recite Words	Students Listen to the Definitions
ceased	Stopped or halted.
morsel	A small piece of food.
labor	Work.
lender	One who allows something to be used by someone else, on the condition it or something equal to it will be returned.
tender	Loving, gentle, or sweet.
distress	To cause discomfort or anxiety.
glummer	More sullen, moody, or sour.

REVIEW QUESTIONS

1. What is the title of the poem?
2. What happens in the poem?
3. What is the setting of the poem?
4. Who are the characters in the poem?
5. What does the poem teach the reader?

TRACEWORK AND/OR COPYWORK

Dance for your bread

DRAW THE POEM (Illustrate an ant saving food for winter.)

LESSON 3: "THE CAT AND THE FOX" BY JEAN DE LA FONTAINE

FEATURED POEM

The Cat and the Fox once took a walk together,
Sharpening their wits with talk about the weather
And as their walking sharpened appetite, too;
They also took some things they had no right to.
Cream, that is so delicious when it thickens,
Pleased the Cat best. The Fox liked little chickens.

With stomachs filled, they presently grew prouder,
And each began to try to talk the louder-
Bragging about his skill, and strength, and cunning.
"Pooh!" said the Fox. "You ought to see me running.
Besides, I have a hundred tricks. You Cat, you!
What can you do when Mr. Dog comes at you?"
"To tell the truth," the Cat said, "though it grieve me
I've but one trick. Yet that's enough-believe me!"

There came a pack of fox-hounds-yelping, baying.
"Pardon me", said the Cat. "I can't be staying.
This is my trick." And up a tree he scurried,
Leaving the Fox below a trifle worried.

In vain he tried his hundred tricks and ruses
(The sort of thing that Mr. Dog confuses)-
Doubling, and seeking one hole, then another-
Smoked out of each until he thought he'd smother.
At last as he once more came out of cover,
Two nimble dogs pounced on him-All was over!

SYNOPSIS

A cat and fox take things that don't belong to them. The fox brags about knowing many tricks, while the cat knows only one trick. When dogs chase the cat and fox, the cat's one trick of climbing a tree saves him, while the fox's many tricks fail him.

ENRICHMENT ACTIVITIES

1. **Recite Poem Information**
   Practice reciting the title of the poem and the name of the poet.

2. **Narrate the Poem**
   Verbally recount poem events in your own words.

3. **Study the Poem Picture**
   Study the poem picture and describe how it relates to the poem.

4. **Can You Find It?**
   Find the following in the poem picture: Fox, cat, tree, and the animal performing the "right" trick.

5. **Act Out the Poem**
   - Use your hands as puppets to act out the poem.
   - Show the cat climbing a tree and escaping from the dogs.
   - Act out the fox trying all of his tricks, and the dogs still catching the fox.

6. **Discuss the Poem**
   Discuss whether it is more important to know the right thing at the right time versus knowing many unhelpful things.

7. **Explore Rhyming**
   Find and recite the rhyming words in the poem.

VOCABULARY

Students Recite Words	Students Listen to the Definitions
cunning	Sly, crafty, or clever.
pooh	Expression of dismissal or contempt.
baying	Barking or howling.
scurried	Ran with quick, light steps.
trifle	A little bit.
ruses	Tricks.
smoked	Driven out using smoke.
smother	To suffocate or stifle the breathing of something or someone.
nimble	Quick and light in movement or action.

REVIEW QUESTIONS

1. What is the title of the poem?
2. What happens in the poem?
3. What is the setting of the poem?
4. Who are the characters in the poem?
5. What does the poem teach the reader?

TRACEWORK AND/OR COPYWORK

"I've one trick," said the Cat.

"Pooh," said the Fox.

"I have a hundred tricks."

ELEMENTARY POETRY VOLUME 2: POETRY OF FABLES, FAIRIES, AND FAUNA

DRAW THE POEM (Sketch a fox performing a trick.)

LESSON 4: "THE DOG AND HIS IMAGE" BY JEAN DE LA FONTAINE

FEATURED POEM

A foolish Dog, who carried in his jaw
A juicy bone,
Looked down into a stream, and there he saw
Another one,
Splash! In he plunged... The image disappeared-
The meat he had was gone.
Indeed, he nearly sank,
And barely reached the bank.

SYNOPSIS

A dog holding a bone in his mouth sees his reflection. Feeling greedy, he tries to grab the bone from his reflection and loses his bone in the water.

ENRICHMENT ACTIVITIES

1. **Recite Poem Information**
   Practice reciting the title of the poem and the name of the poet.
2. **Narrate the Poem**
   Verbally recount poem events in your own words.
3. **Study the Poem Picture**
   Study the poem picture and describe how it relates to the poem.
4. **Can You Find It?**
   Find the following in the poem picture: Dog, bone, dog reflection, bone reflection, stream, and cattails.
5. **Act Out the Poem**
   - Act out the greedy dog and the events of the poem.
   - Roll up a piece of paper to use as a bone.
   - Holding the "bone" up to a mirror, try to take the bone from your reflection.
6. **Discuss the Poem**
   Discuss how the old saying, "a bird in the hand is worth two in the bush," relates to the poem.
7. **Explore Rhyming**
   Find and recite the rhyming words in the poem.

VOCABULARY

Students Recite Words	Students Listen to the Definitions
foolish	Lacking good sense or judgement; unwise.
jaw	One of the bones of the mouth, usually bearing teeth.
juicy	Having lots of juice.
plunged	Dove, jumped, or rushed into water.
image	A picture of something not real or not present.
disappeared	Went away or vanished.
sank	Moved down under the water.
bank	The land along a river.

REVIEW QUESTIONS

1. What is the title of the poem?
2. What happens in the poem?
3. What is the setting of the poem?
4. Who are the characters in the poem?
5. What does the poem teach the reader?

TRACEWORK AND/OR COPYWORK

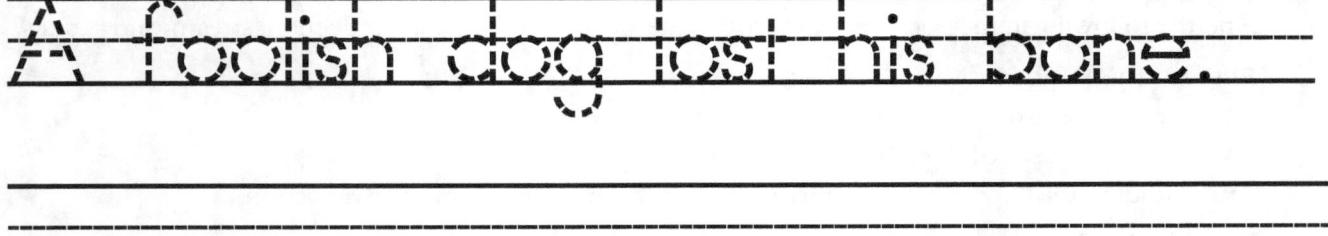

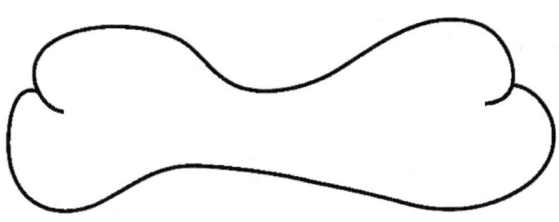

DRAW THE POEM (Depict a dog's reflection in a stream or lake.)

LESSON 5: "THE RAVEN AND THE FOX" BY JEAN DE LA FONTAINE

FEATURED POEM

Mr. Raven was perched upon a limb,
And Reynard the Fox looked up at him;
For the Raven held in his great big beak
A morsel the Fox would go far to seek.

Said the Fox, in admiring tones: "My word!
Sir Raven, you are a handsome bird.
Such feathers! If you would only sing,
The birds of these woods would call you King."

The Raven, who did not see the joke,
Forgot that his voice was just a croak.
He opened his beak, in his foolish pride-
And down fell the morsel the Fox had spied.

"Ha-ha!" said the Fox. "And now you see
You should not listen to flattery.
Vanity, sir is a horrid vice-
I'm sure the lesson is worth the price."

SYNOPSIS

A raven in a tree holds a tasty treat in his beak that a fox would like to eat. The fox falsely flatters the bird, inciting the raven to sing, even though ravens make ugly caws. When the raven squawks, the tasty morsel falls into the fox's mouth.

ENRICHMENT ACTIVITIES

1. **Recite Poem Information**
   Practice reciting the title of the poem and the name of the poet.
2. **Narrate the Poem**
   Verbally recount poem events in your own words.
3. **Study the Poem Picture**
   Study the poem picture and describe how it relates to the poem.
4. **Can You Find It?**
   Find the following in the poem picture: Raven, fox, beak, morsel, and feathers.
5. **Act Out the Poem**
   - Use your hands as puppets to act out the fox and the raven from the poem.
   - Show the fox flattering the raven as the raven holds a morsel (piece of paper) in her mouth.
   - Next show the raven squawking and dropping her morsel.
   - Finally, have the fox gobble up the delicious dropped morsel.
6. **Discuss the Poem**
   - Discuss why or why not the raven should have believed the fox's flattery.
   - If a stranger is overly nice and flattering to you, should you trust them or should you be wary?
7. **Explore Rhyming**
   Find and recite the rhyming words in the poem.

VOCABULARY

Students Recite Words	Students Listen to the Definitions
limb	A branch of a tree.
morsel	A small piece of food.
admiring	Being amazed at or marveling at.
croak	A faint, harsh sound made in the throat.
spied	Seen or spotted.
vanity	Excessive pride in or admiration of one's own abilities, appearance, or achievements.
horrid	Awful, offensive, disagreeable, or abominable.
vice	A bad habit.

REVIEW QUESTIONS

1. What is the title of the poem?
2. What happens in the poem?
3. What is the setting of the poem?
4. Who are the characters in the poem?
5. What does the poem teach the reader?

TRACEWORK AND/OR COPYWORK

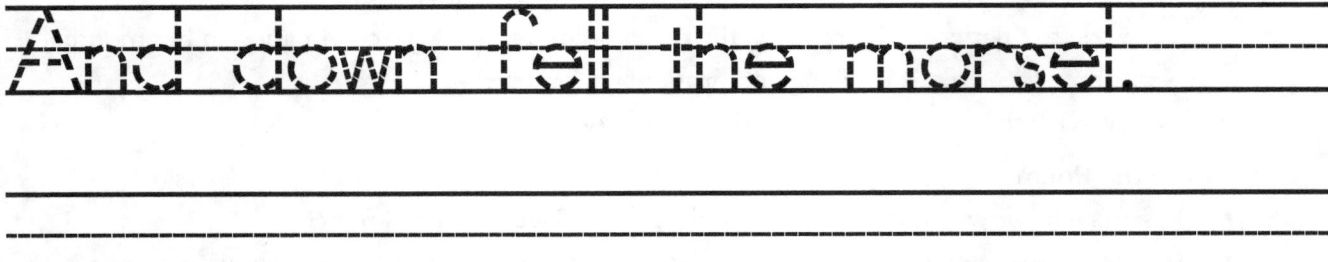

And down fell the morsel.

DRAW THE POEM (Complete and color the outline of the crow.)

LESSON 6: "THE CITY MOUSE AND THE COUNTRY MOUSE" BY JEAN DE LA FONTAINE

FEATURED POEM

A City Mouse, with ways polite,
A Country Mouse invited
To sup with him and spend the night.
Said Country Mouse: "De-lighted!"
In truth it proved a royal treat,
With everything that's good to eat.

Alas! When they had just begun
To gobble their dinner,
A knock was heard that made them run.
The City Mouse seemed thinner.
And as they scampered and turned tail,
He saw the Country Mouse grow pale.

The knocking ceased. A false alarm!
The City Mouse grew braver.
"Come back!" he cried. "No, no! The farm,
Where I'll not quake or quaver,
Suits me," replied the Country Mouse.
"You're welcome to your city house."

SYNOPSIS

A country mouse visits a city mouse and samples the delicious foods the city has to offer. When they hear a noise, the country mouse flees back to the country, valuing safety and serenity over decadence.

ENRICHMENT ACTIVITIES

1. **Recite Poem Information**
   Practice reciting the title of the poem and the name of the poet.
2. **Narrate the Poem**
   Verbally recount poem events in your own words.

3. **Study the Poem Picture**
   Study the poem picture and describe how it relates to the poem.

4. **Can You Find It?**
   Find the following in the poem picture: City mouse, country mouse, fruit, candelabra, cheese, glass, and knife.

5. **Discuss the Poem**
   Discuss whether you agree with the country mouse – that peace of mind is more important than luxuries such as fine food.

6. **Explore Rhyming**
   Find and recite the rhyming words in the poem.

VOCABULARY

Students Recite Words	Students Listen to the Definitions
polite	Well-mannered, civilized.
sup	To take supper.
royal	Worthy of a king or other member of a monarchy.
gobble	To eat quickly or greedily.
false alarm	A warning that turns out to be false.
quaver	A trembling shake.
suits	To be appropriate for.

REVIEW QUESTIONS

1. What is the title of the poem?

2. What happens in the poem?

3. What is the setting of the poem?

4. Who are the characters in the poem?

5. What does the poem teach the reader?

TRACEWORK AND/OR COPYWORK

The farm life suits me.

DRAW THE POEM (Depict a happy mouse playing in the country.)

LESSON 7: "THE DOVE AND THE ANT" BY JEAN DE LA FONTAINE

FEATURED POEM

An Ant who in a brook would drink
Fell off the bank. He tried
To swim, and felt his courage sink-
This ocean seemed so wide.
But for a dove who flew above
He would have drowned and died.

The friendly Dove within her beak
A bridge of grass-stem bore:
On this the Ant, though worn and weak.
Contrived to reach the shore
Said he: "The tact of this kind act
I'll cherish evermore."

Behold! A barefoot wretch went by
With slingshot in his hand.
Said he: "You'll make a pigeon pie
That will be kind of grand."
He meant to murder the gentle bird-
Who did not understand.

The Ant then stung him on the heel
(So quick to see the sling).
He turned his head, and missed a meal:
The pigeon pie took wing.
And so the Dove lived on to love-
Beloved by everything.

SYNOPSIS

A dove rescues an ant from drowning. Later, the ant rescues the dove from a boy with a slingshot.

ENRICHMENT ACTIVITIES

1. **Recite Poem Information**
   Practice reciting the title of the poem and the name of the poet.
2. **Narrate the Poem**
   Verbally recount poem events in your own words.
3. **Study the Poem Picture**
   Study the poem picture and describe how it relates to the poem.
4. **Can You Find It?**
   Find the following in the poem picture: Dove, ant, brook, grass, tree, and shore.
5. **Discuss the Poem**
   - Discuss the dove's selfless act.
   - Discuss how the dove's selfless act benefitted her in the long run.
   - Have you ever performed a selfless act? If so, what was it?
6. **Explore Rhyming**
   Find and recite the rhyming words in the poem.

VOCABULARY

Students Recite Words	Students Listen to the Definitions
brook	A body of running water smaller than a river; a small stream.
courage	The ability to do things which one finds frightening.
tact	Careful consideration in dealing with others to avoid giving offense.
cherish	To hold dear or to treat with tenderness.
wretch	An unhappy, unfortunate, or miserable person.
slingshot	A Y-shaped stick with an elastic sling between the arms used for shooting small projectiles.

REVIEW QUESTIONS

1. What is the title of the poem?
2. What happens in the poem?
3. Where does the poem take place?
4. Who are the characters in the poem?
5. What does the poem teach the reader?

TRACEWORK AND/OR COPYWORK

The ant stung the wretch.

DRAW THE POEM (Illustrate the ant stinging the boy.)

LESSON 8: "THE FOX AND THE GRAPES" BY JEAN DE LA FONTAINE

FEATURED POEM

Rosy and ripe, and ready to box,
The grapes hang high o'er the hungry Fox.-
He pricks up his ears, and his eye he cocks.

Ripe and rosy, yet so high!-
He gazes at them with a greedy eye,
And knows he must eat and drink-or die.

When the jump proves to be beyond his power-
"Pooh!" says the Fox. "Let the pigs devour
Fruit of that sort. Those grapes are sour!"

SYNOPSIS

A fox tries to reach some grapes, but they are too high. Irked by his failure, the fox claims the grapes are sour and he doesn't really want them anyway.

ENRICHMENT ACTIVITIES

1. **Recite Poem Information**
   Practice reciting the title of the poem and the name of the poet.
2. **Narrate the Poem**
   Verbally recount poem events in your own words.
3. **Study the Poem Picture**
   Study the poem picture and describe how it relates to the poem.
4. **Can You Find It?**
   Find the following in the poem picture: Fox, grapes, tree, leaves, vines, grass, mountain, and clouds.
8. **Act Out the Poem**
   - Pretend to be the fox leaping up to reach the grapes.
   - Pout and sulk when you cannot get the grapes and say, "I don't want those sour grapes!"
5. **Explore Rhyming**
   Find and recite the rhyming words in the poem.

VOCABULARY

Students Recite Words	Students Listen to the Definitions
ripe	Ready for reaping or gathering; having attained perfection; mature.
greedy	Having a selfish desire for more than is needed.
pooh	Expression of dismissal or contempt.
devour	To eat quickly, greedily, hungrily, or ravenously.
sour	Having an acidic, sharp, or tangy taste.

REVIEW QUESTIONS

1. What is the title of the poem?
2. What happens in the poem?
3. Where does the poem take place?
4. Who are the characters in the poem?
5. What does the poem teach the reader?

TRACEWORK AND/OR COPYWORK

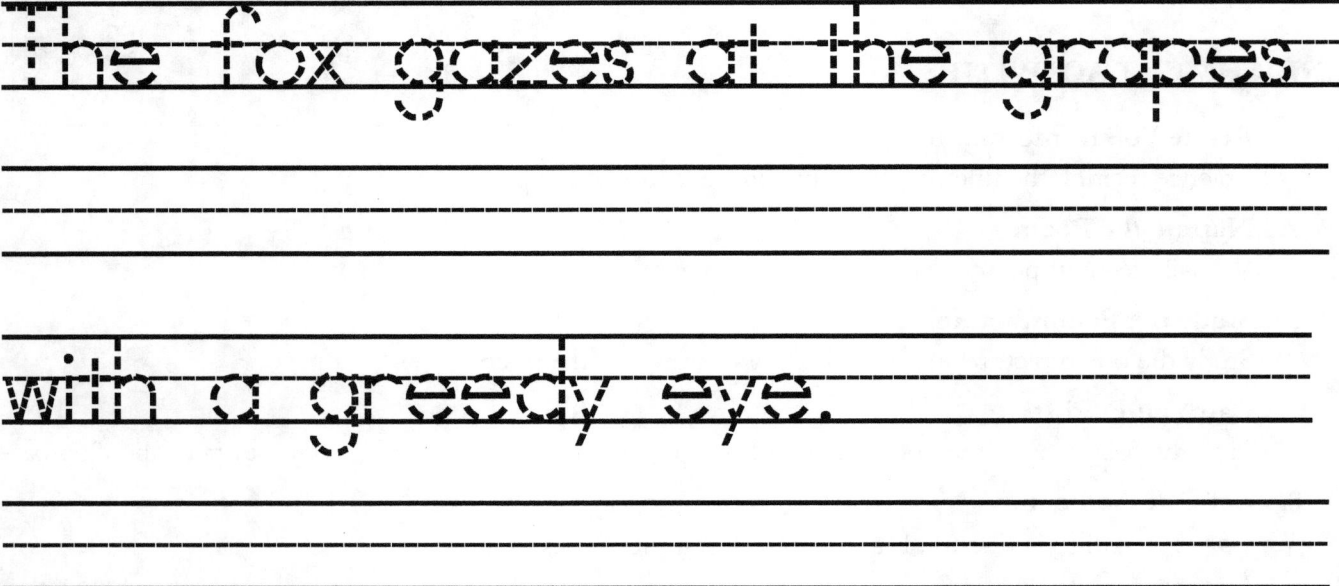

DRAW THE POEM (Sketch and color a big bunch of juicy grapes.)

LESSON 9: "THE FOX AND THE STORK" BY JEAN DE LA FONTAINE

FEATURED POEM

1. Old Father Fox, who was known to be mean,
Invited Dame Stork in to dinner.
There was nothing but soup that could scarcely be seen:-
Soup never was served any thinner.
And the worst of it was, as I'm bound to relate,
Father Fox dished it up on a flat china plate.

2. Dame Stork, as you know, has a very long beak:
Not a crumb or drop could she gather
Had she pecked at the plate every day in the week.
But as for the Fox-sly old Father:
With his tongue lapping soup at a scandalous rate,
He licked up the last little bit and polished the plate.

3. Pretty soon Mistress Stork spread a feast of her own;
Father Fox was invited to share it.
He came, and he saw, and he gave a great groan:
The stork had known how to prepare it.
She had meant to get even, and now was her turn:
Father Fox was invited to eat from an urn.

4. The urn's mouth was small, and it had a long neck;
The food in it smelled most delightful.
Dame Stork, with her beak in, proceeded to peck;
But the Fox found that fasting is frightful.
Home he sneaked. On his way there he felt his ears burn
When he thought of the Stork and her tall, tricky urn.

SYNOPSIS

A fox invites a stork to dinner and serves soup on a plate, making it impossible for the stork to eat. In return, the stork invites the fox to dinner and serves food in an urn, making it impossible for the fox to eat.

ENRICHMENT ACTIVITIES

1. **Recite Poem Information**
   Practice reciting the title of the poem and the name of the poet.
2. **Narrate the Poem**
   Verbally recount poem events in your own words.
3. **Study the Poem Pictures**
   Study the poem pictures and describe how they relate to the poem.
4. **Can You Find It?**
   Find the following in the poem pictures: Fox, stork, plate, soup, and urn.
5. **Make a Wearable Beak Mask**
   - Cut two large equally-sized triangles out of orange construction paper and partially fold them.
   - Bend out the outer edges so you can glue or tape the triangles together to form a beak.
   - Cut small holes on either side of the beak and tie string or dental floss between the holes so you can wear the beak as a mask.
   - Pour some water on a plate.
   - Like the stork attempting to drink soup in the poem, try to drink from the plate.
   - Can you drink the water without bending or removing your beak?
6. **Explore Rhyming**
   Find and recite the rhyming words in the poem.

VOCABULARY

Students Recite Words	Students Listen to the Definitions
scarcely	Barely or hardly.
thinner	More dilute or more watery.
sly	Artfully cunning, secretly mischievous, or sly.
scandalous	Causing an incident or event that disgraces or damages the reputation of the persons or organization involved.
polished	Made smooth or shiny.
urn	A vase with a footed base.
fasting	Abstaining from eating food.

ELEMENTARY POETRY VOLUME 2: POETRY OF FABLES, FAIRIES, AND FAUNA

REVIEW QUESTIONS

1. What is the title of the poem?
2. What happens in the poem?
3. Where does the poem take place?
4. Who are the characters in the poem?
5. What does the poem teach the reader?

TRACEWORK AND/OR COPYWORK

She had meant to get even,

and now was her turn.

Father Fox was invited to eat

from an urn.

DRAW THE POEM (Decorate the urn.)

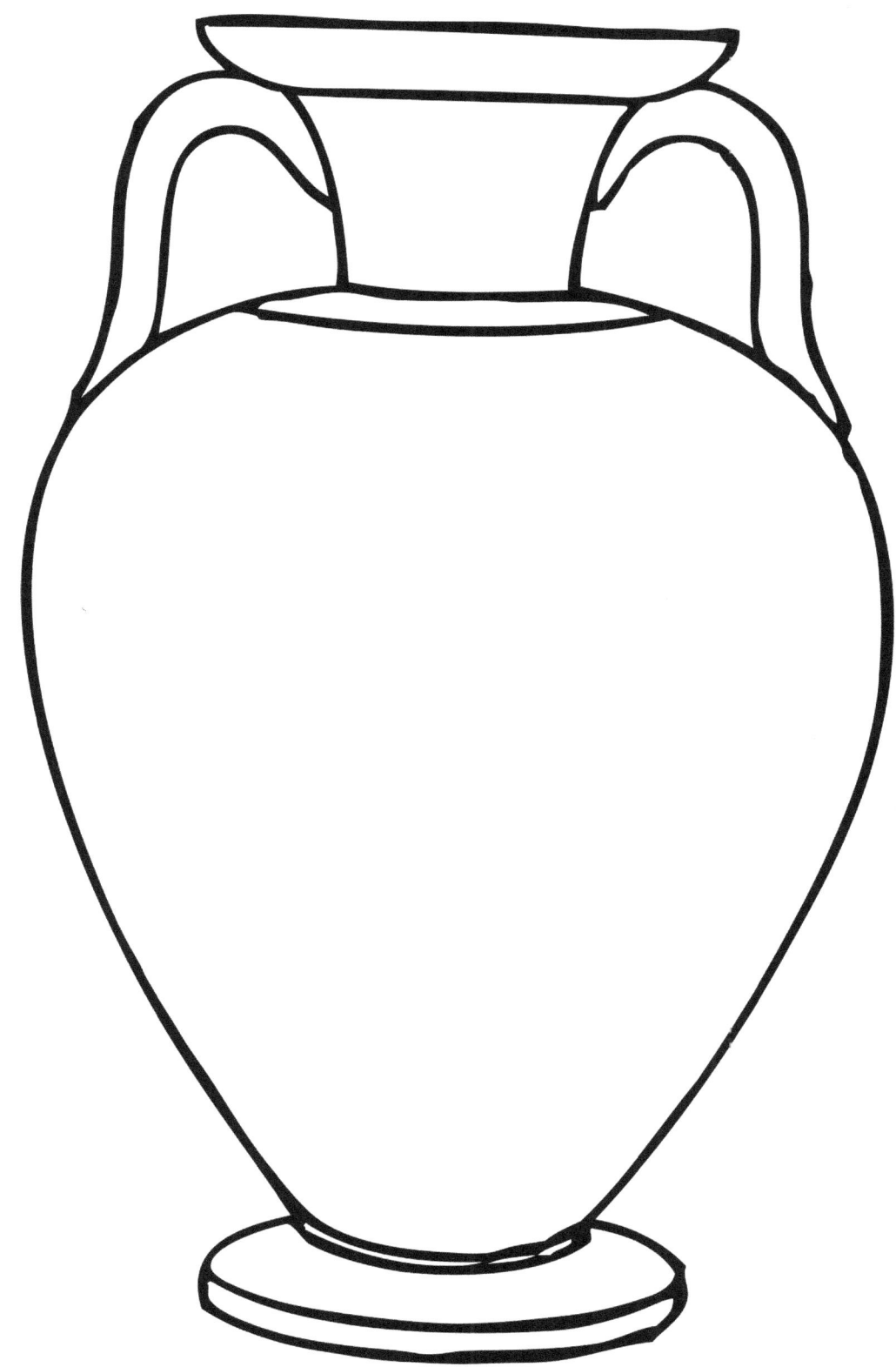

LESSON 10: "THE HARE AND THE TORTOISE" BY JEAN DE LA FONTAINE

FEATURED POEM

Said the Tortoise one day to the Hare:
"I'll run you a race if you dare.
I'll bet you cannot
Arrive at that spot
As quickly as I can get there."

Quoth the Hare: "You are surely insane.
Pray, what has affected your brain?
You seem pretty sick.
Call a doctor in-quick,
And let him prescribe for your pain."

"Never mind," said the Tortoise. "Let's run!
Will you bet me?" "Why, certainly." "Done!"
While the slow Tortoise creeps
Mr. Hare makes four leaps,
And then loafs around in the sun.

It seemed such a one-sided race,
To win was almost a disgrace.
So he frolicked about
Then at last he set out-
As the Tortoise was as nearing the place.

Too late! Though he sped like a dart,
The Tortoise was first. She was smart:
"You can surely run fast,"
She remarked. "Yet you're last.
It is better to get a good start."

SYNOPSIS

A hare and a tortoise race. Even though the hare is far faster, he suffers from overconfidence, doesn't try his hardest, and the tortoise wins the race.

ENRICHMENT ACTIVITIES

1. **Recite Poem Information**
   Practice reciting the title of the poem and the name of the poet.
2. **Narrate the Poem**
   Verbally recount poem events in your own words.
3. **Study the Poem Picture**
   Study the poem picture and describe how it relates to the poem.
4. **Can You Find It?**
   Find the following in the poem pictures: Tortoise, hare, road, sign, someone fast, and someone slow.
5. **Act Out the Poem**
   - Use your hands as hare and tortoise puppets to act out the race.
   - Show the hare racing in front of the creeping tortoise.
   - Act out the hare loafing around under the sun as the tortoise slowly passes him.
   - Show the hare scrambling to catch up as the tortoise crosses the finish line first to win.
6. **Explore Rhyming**
   Find and recite the rhyming words in the poem.

VOCABULARY

Students Recite Words	Students Listen to the Definitions
insane	Exhibiting unsoundness or disorder of mind; mad.
prescribe	To order a drug or medical device for use by a particular patient.
creeps	Moves slowly with the abdomen close to the ground.
leaps	Jumps.
loafs	Does nothing or is idle.
disgrace	Something which brings dishonor; the cause of shame or reproach.
frolicked	Behaved playfully or merrily.
dart	Any sharp-pointed missile weapon, such as an arrow.

REVIEW QUESTIONS

1. What is the title of the poem?
2. What happens in the poem?
3. Where does the poem take place?
4. Who are the characters in the poem?
5. What does the poem teach the reader?

TRACEWORK AND/OR COPYWORK

I'll bet you cannot

Arrive at that spot

As quickly as I can get there.

DRAW THE POEM (Depict the tortoise crossing the finish line.)

LESSON 11: "THE HERON WHO WAS HARD TO PLEASE" BY JEAN DE LA FONTAINE

FEATURED POEM

A long-legged Heron, with long neck and beak,
Set out for a stroll by the bank of a creek.
So clear was the water that if you looked sharp
You could see the pike caper around with the carp.

The Heron might quickly have speared enough fish
To make for his dinner a capital dish.
But he was a very particular bird:
His food fixed "just so," at the hours he preferred.

And hence he decided 'twas better to wait,
Since his appetite grew when he supped rather late.
Pretty soon he was hungry, and stalked to the bank.
Where some pondfish were leaping-a fish of low rank.

"Bah, Bah!" said the Bird. "Sup on these? No-not I.
I'm known as a Heron: as such I live high."
Then some gudgeon swam past that were tempting to see,
But the Heron said haughtily: "No-not for me.

For those I'd not bother to open my beak,
If I had to hang 'round come next Friday a week."
Thus bragged the big Bird. But he's bound to confess
That he opened his elegant beak for much less.
Not another fish came. When he found all else fail,
He was happy to happen upon a fat snail.

SYNOPSIS

A heron strolls along a creek. He ignores the numerous delicious fish swimming around, waiting until his preferred time to hunt. When he's finally ready to hunt, he disdains pondfish and gudgeon, waiting for something better to swim along. Eventually the fish disappear, and the heron must settle for a snail.

ENRICHMENT ACTIVITIES

1. **Recite Poem Information**
   Practice reciting the title of the poem and the name of the poet.

2. **Narrate the Poem**
   Verbally recount poem events in your own words.

3. **Study the Poem Picture**
   Study the poem picture and describe how it relates to the poem.

4. **Can You Find It?**
   Find the following in the poem pictures: Heron, creek, bank, beak, wings, and claws.

5. **Act Out the Poem**
   Pretend to be the heron, strolling along the creek and disdainfully ignoring any nearby fish.

6. **Explore Rhyming**
   Find and recite the rhyming words in the poem.

VOCABULARY

Students Recite Words	Students Listen to the Definitions
pike	A type of freshwater fish with big teeth and a pointy snout.
caper	A playful leap or jump.
carp	A type of freshwater fish, farmed for food.
capital	Excellent or superb.
gudgeon	A small freshwater fish that is used as bait by fishermen.

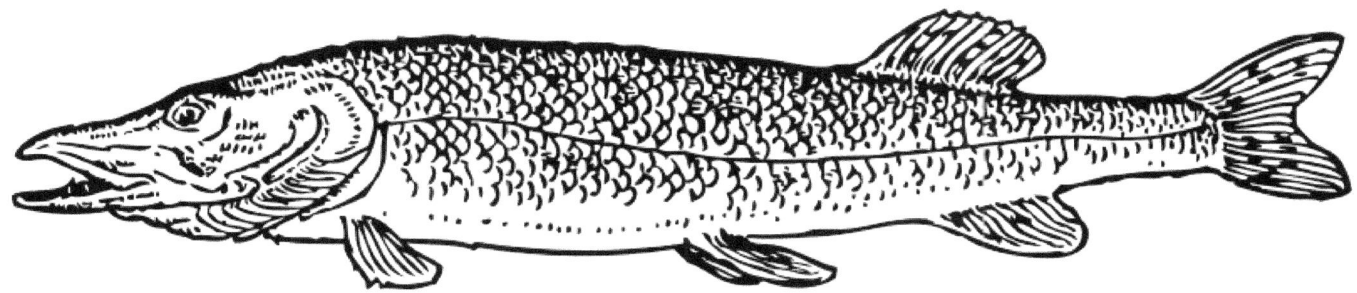

REVIEW QUESTIONS

1. What is the title of the poem?
2. What happens in the poem?
3. Where does the poem take place?
4. Who are the characters in the poem?
5. What does the poem teach the reader?

TRACEWORK AND/OR COPYWORK

Not another fish come.

He was happy to happen

upon a fat snail.

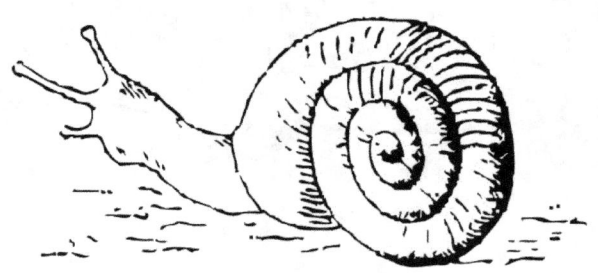

DRAW THE POEM (Illustrate the heron eating a snail.)

LESSON 12: "THE LION AND THE GNAT" BY JEAN DE LA FONTAINE

FEATURED POEM

The Lion once said to the Gnat: "You brat,
Clear out just as quick as you can, now-s'cat!
If you meddle with me
I will not guarantee
That you won't be slammed perfectly flat-
D'ye see?"

Said the Gnat: "Because you're called King-you thing!
You fancy that you will make me take wing.
Why, an ox weighs much more,
Yet I drive him before
When I get good and ready to sting.
Now, roar!"

Then loudly his trumpet he blew. And-whew!
How fiercely and fast at his foe he flew.
From the tail to the toes
He draws blood as he goes.
Then he starts in to sting and to chew
His nose.

Sir Lion was mad with the pain. In vain
He roared and he foamed and he shook his mane.
All the beasts that were nigh
Fled in fear from his cry.
But the Gnat only stung him again-
In the eye.

He looked and laughed as he saw-Haw, Haw!-
The Lion self-torn by his tooth and claw,
So His Majesty's hide
With his own blood was dyed.
Said the Gnat: "Shall I serve you up raw-
Or fried?"

It's finished. The Lion's loud roar is o'er.
He's bitten and beaten, he's sick and sore.
But a spider's web spread
Trapped the Gnat as he sped
With the news...He will never fight more-
He's dead!

SYNOPSIS

A gnat mocks and stings a lion, turning the lion's strength against himself. The sassy gnat gets his comeuppance when he becomes entangled in a web and is eaten by a spider.

ENRICHMENT ACTIVITIES

1. **Recite Poem Information**
   Practice reciting the title of the poem and the name of the poet.
2. **Narrate the Poem**
   Verbally recount poem events in your own words.
3. **Study the Poem Pictures**
   Study the poem pictures and describe how they relate to the poem.
4. **Can You Find It?**
   Find the following in the poem pictures: Lion, gnat, spider, and spiderweb.
5. **Act Out the Poem**
   - Pretend to be the gnat ensnared in the spider's web.
   - Struggle and show fear as the spider approaches you.
6. **Explore Rhyming**
   Find and recite the rhyming words in the poem.

VOCABULARY

Students Recite Words	Students Listen to the Definitions
meddle	To interfere in or with.
foe	An enemy.
nigh	Near, close by.

REVIEW QUESTIONS

1. What is the title of the poem?
2. What happens in the poem?
3. Where does the poem take place?
4. Who are the characters in the poem?
5. What does the poem teach the reader?

TRACEWORK AND/OR COPYWORK

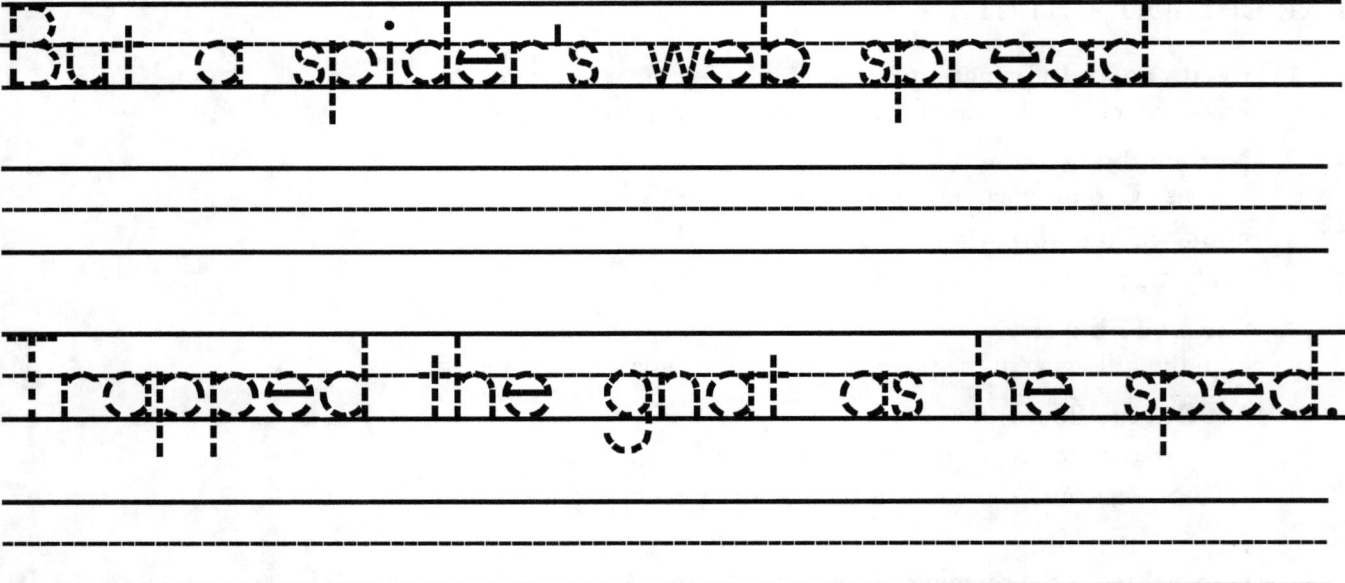

DRAW THE POEM (Depict a spider approaching a trapped gnat.)

PART II: POETRY OF FAIRIES
LESSON 13. "THE FAIRIES"
BY WILLIAM ALLINGHAM

FEATURED POEM

1. Up the airy mountain,
Down the rushy glen,
We daren't go a-hunting
For fear of little men;
Wee folk, good folk,
Trooping all together;
Green jacket, red cap,
And white owl's feather!

2. Down along the rocky shore
Some make their home,
They live on crispy pancakes
Of yellow tide-foam;
Some in the reeds
Of the black mountain-lake,
With frogs for their watch-dogs,
All night awake.

3. High on the hill-top
The old King sits;
He is now so old and gray
He's nigh lost his wits.
With a bridge of white mist
Columbkill he crosses,
On his stately journeys
From Slieveleague to Rosses;
Or going up with music
On cold starry nights,
To sup with the Queen
Of the gay Northern Lights.

4. They stole little Bridget
For seven years long;
When she came down again
Her friends were all gone.
They took her lightly back,
Between the night and morrow,
They thought that she was fast asleep,
But she was dead with sorrow.
They have kept her ever since
Deep within the lake,
On a bed of flag-leaves,
Watching till she wake.

5. By the craggy hill-side,
Through the mosses bare,
They have planted thorn-trees
For pleasure here and there.
Is any man so daring
As dig them up in spite,
He shall find their sharpest thorns
In his bed at night.

6. Up the airy mountain,
Down the rushy glen,
We daren't go a-hunting
For fear of little men;
Wee folk, good folk,
Trooping all together;
Green jacket, red cap,
And white owl's feather!

SYNOPSIS

The poem describes the lives and hijinks of a group of fairies, including their king and queen. They scare hunters, plant trees, steal children, and get revenge.

ENRICHMENT ACTIVITIES

1. **Recite Poem Information**
   Practice reciting the title of the poem and the name of the poet.
2. **Narrate the Poem**
   Verbally recount poem events in your own words.
3. **Study the Poem Pictures**
   Study the poem pictures and describe how they relate to the poem.
4. **Can You Find It?**
   Find the following in the poem pictures: Fairies, wings, frog, feather, mountains, and glen.
5. **Act Out the Poem**
   - Pretend to be a fairy sneaking into a house.
   - Steal little Bridget and abscond with her to the land of the fairies.
6. **Explore Rhyming**
   Find and recite the rhyming words in the poem.

VOCABULARY

Students Recite Words	Students Listen to the Definitions
glen	A narrow valley.
tide	The alternate rising and falling of the sea, usually twice in each lunar day at a particular place, due to the attraction of the moon and sun.
Columbkill	A former civil parish (small territorial area) in Ireland.
Slieveleague	A mountain in Ireland on the Atlantic coast.
Rosses	A region in Ireland.
northern lights	A natural electrical phenomenon characterized by the appearance of streamers of reddish or greenish light in the sky, usually near the northern or southern magnetic pole.
craggy	Rough and uneven (cliff or rock face).
thorn-trees	A tree with thorny leaves.

REVIEW QUESTIONS

1. What is the title of the poem?
2. What happens in the poem?
3. Where does the poem take place?
4. Who are the characters in the poem?
5. What does the poem teach the reader?

TRACEWORK AND/OR COPYWORK

Up the airy mountain,

Down the rushy glen,

We daren't go a-hunting

For fear of little men

DRAW THE POEM (Color a fairy in a green coat and a red cap.)

LESSON 14: "THE ELF SINGING"
BY WILLIAM ALLINGHAM

FEATURED POEM

1. An Elf sat on a twig,
He was not very big,
He sang a little song,
He did not think it wrong;
But he was on a Wizard's ground,
Who hated all sweet sound.

2. Elf, Elf,
Take care of yourself!
He's coming behind you,
To seize you and bind you,
And stifle your song.

3. The Wizard! the Wizard!
He changes his shape
In crawling along,
An ugly old ape,
A poisonous lizard,

4. A spotted spider,
A wormy glider,
The Wizard! the Wizard!
He's up on the bough,
He'll bite through your gizzard
He's close to you now!

5. The Elf went on with his song,
It grew more clear and strong,
It lifted him into air,
He floated singing away,
With rainbows in his hair;
While the Wizard-worm from his creep

6. Made a sudden leap,
Fell down into a hole,
And, ere his magic word he could say,
Was eaten up by a Mole.

SYNOPSIS

The poem tells the tale of a wizard that transforms into a snake and tries to eat a fairy. The fairy's song uplifts him and saves him while the wizard falls and is eaten by a mole.

ENRICHMENT ACTIVITIES

1. **Recite Poem Information**
   Practice reciting the title of the poem and the name of the poet.
2. **Narrate the Poem**
   Verbally recount poem events in your own words.
3. **Study the Poem Picture**
   Study the poem picture and describe how it relates to the poem.
4. **Can You Find It?**
   Find the following in the poem picture: Fairy, wings, and bough.
5. **Act Out the Poem**
   - Pretend to be the wizard in snake form sneakily slithering over the tree bough toward the fairy.
   - As you attempt to strike the fairy, you fall and are eaten by the mole.
6. **Explore Rhyming**
   Find and recite the rhyming words in the poem.

VOCABULARY

Students Recite Words	Students Listen to the Definitions
elf	A supernatural creature of folk tales, typically represented as a small, elusive figure in human form with pointed ears, magical powers, and a capricious nature.
twig	A slender woody shoot growing from a branch or stem of a tree or shrub.
seize	Take hold of suddenly and forcibly.
bind	Tie or fasten something tightly.
bough	A main branch of a tree.
gizzard	A person's stomach or throat.
mole	A small burrowing mammal with dark velvety fur, a long muzzle, and very small eyes.
meadow	A piece of grassland or low ground near a river.

ELEMENTARY POETRY VOLUME 2: POETRY OF FABLES, FAIRIES, AND FAUNA

REVIEW QUESTIONS

1. What is the title of the poem?
2. What happens in the poem?
3. Where does the poem take place?
4. Who are the characters in the poem?
5. What does the poem teach the reader?

TRACEWORK AND/OR COPYWORK

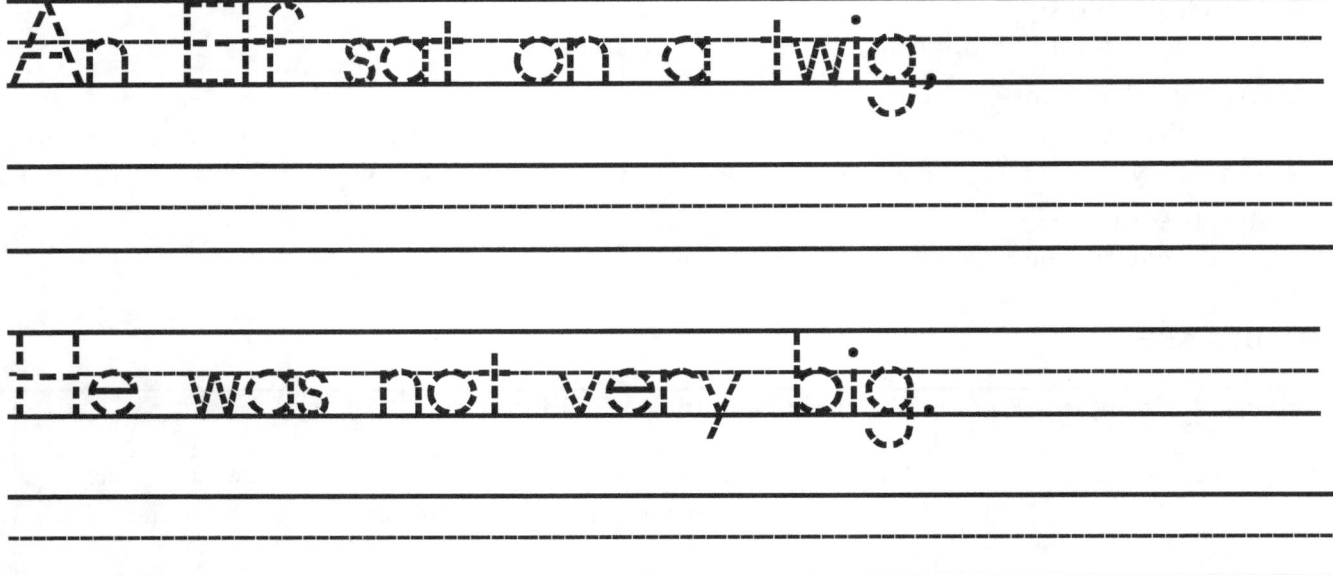

An Elf sat on a twig,

He was not very big.

DRAW THE POEM (Sketch a snake sneaking along a tree bough.)

LESSON 15: "THE FAIRY KING"
WILLIAM ALLINGHAM

FEATURED POEM

High on the hill-top
The old King sits;
He is now so old and gray
He's nigh lost his wits."

The Fairy King was old.
He met the Witch of the Wold.
"Ah ha, King!" quoth she,
"Now thou art old like me."
"Nay, Witch!" quoth he,
"I am not old like thee."

The King took off his crown,
It almost bent him down;
His age was too great
To carry such a weight.
"Give it here!" she said,
And clapt it on her head.

Crown sank to ground;
The Witch no more was found.
Then sweet spring-songs were sung,
The Fairy King grew young,
His crown was made of flowers,
He lived in woods and bowers.

SYNOPSIS

The Witch of the Wold grabs the old Fairy King's crown and puts it on her head. In a twist, stealing and wearing the crown vanquishes the witch. She disappears, and the king grows young.

ENRICHMENT ACTIVITIES

1. **Recite Poem Information**
   Practice reciting the title of the poem and the name of the poet.

2. **Narrate the Poem**
   Verbally recount poem events in your own words.

3. **Study the Poem Picture**
   Study the poem picture and describe how it relates to the poem.

4. **Can You Find It?**
   Find the following in the poem pictures: Witch, king, crown, and someone who disappears.

5. **Act Out the Poem**
   - Pretend to be the witch stealing the king's crown and placing it upon your head.
   - Shriek as you disappear under the crown and sink into the ground.

6. **Explore Rhyming**
   Find and recite the rhyming words in the poem.

VOCABULARY

Students Recite Words	Students Listen to the Definitions
nigh	Near or almost.
wits	Mental sharpness.
wold	A piece of high, open, uncultivated land.
quoth	Another word for "said."
thou	Another word for "you."
art	Another word for "are."
clapt	Placed or put.
bower	A pleasant shady place under trees or plants in a garden or wood.

REVIEW QUESTIONS

1. What is the title of the poem?

2. What happens in the poem?

3. Where does the poem take place?

4. Who are the characters in the poem?

5. What does the poem teach the reader?

TRACEWORK AND/OR COPYWORK

High on the hill-top

The old King sits;

He is now so old and gray

He's nigh lost his wits.

DRAW THE POEM (Color the young king's crown of flowers, adding your own embellishments.)

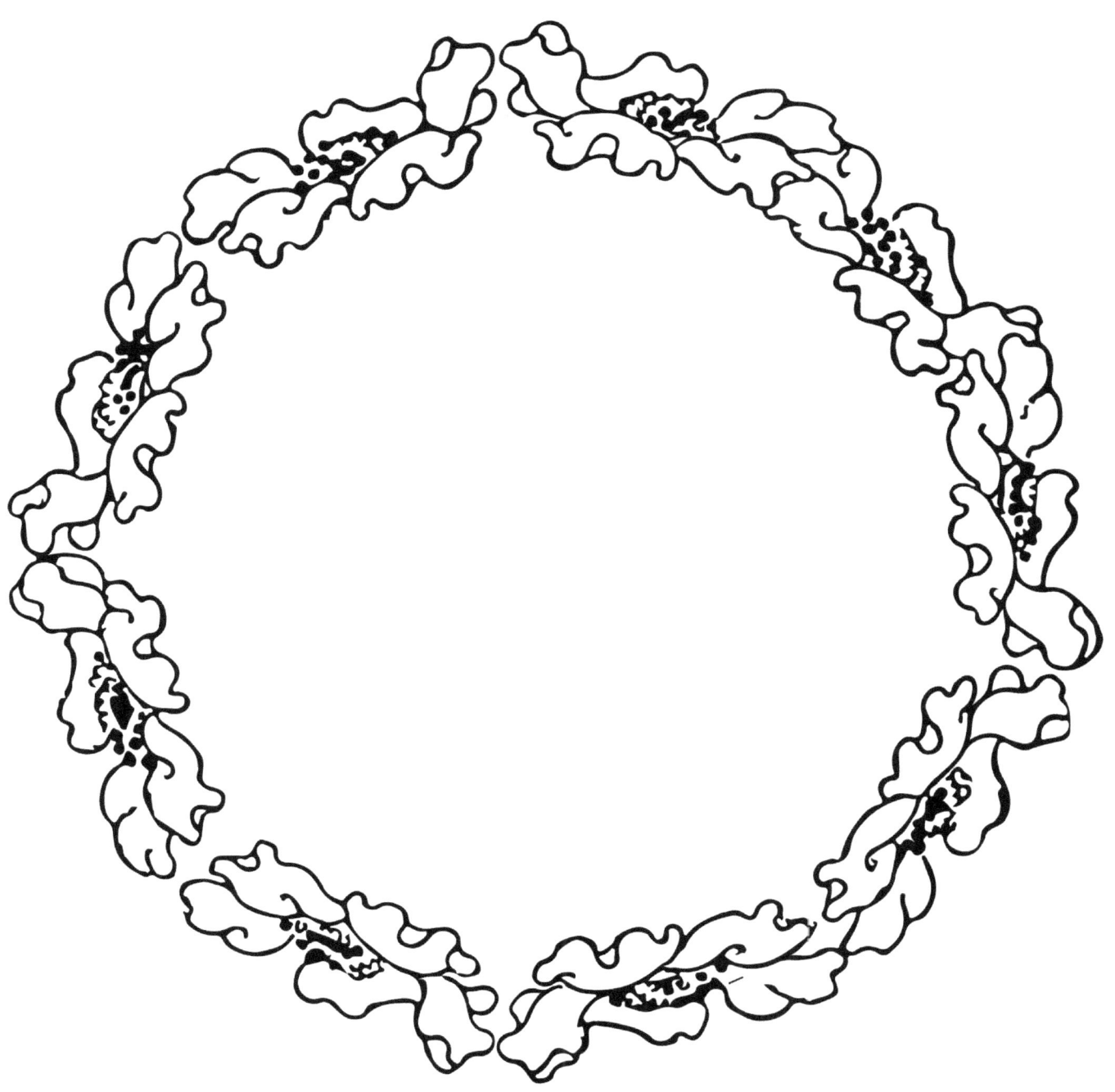

ELEMENTARY POETRY VOLUME 2: POETRY OF FABLES, FAIRIES, AND FAUNA

LESSON 16: "CHORUS OF FAIRIES" BY WILLIAM ALLINGHAM

FEATURED POEM

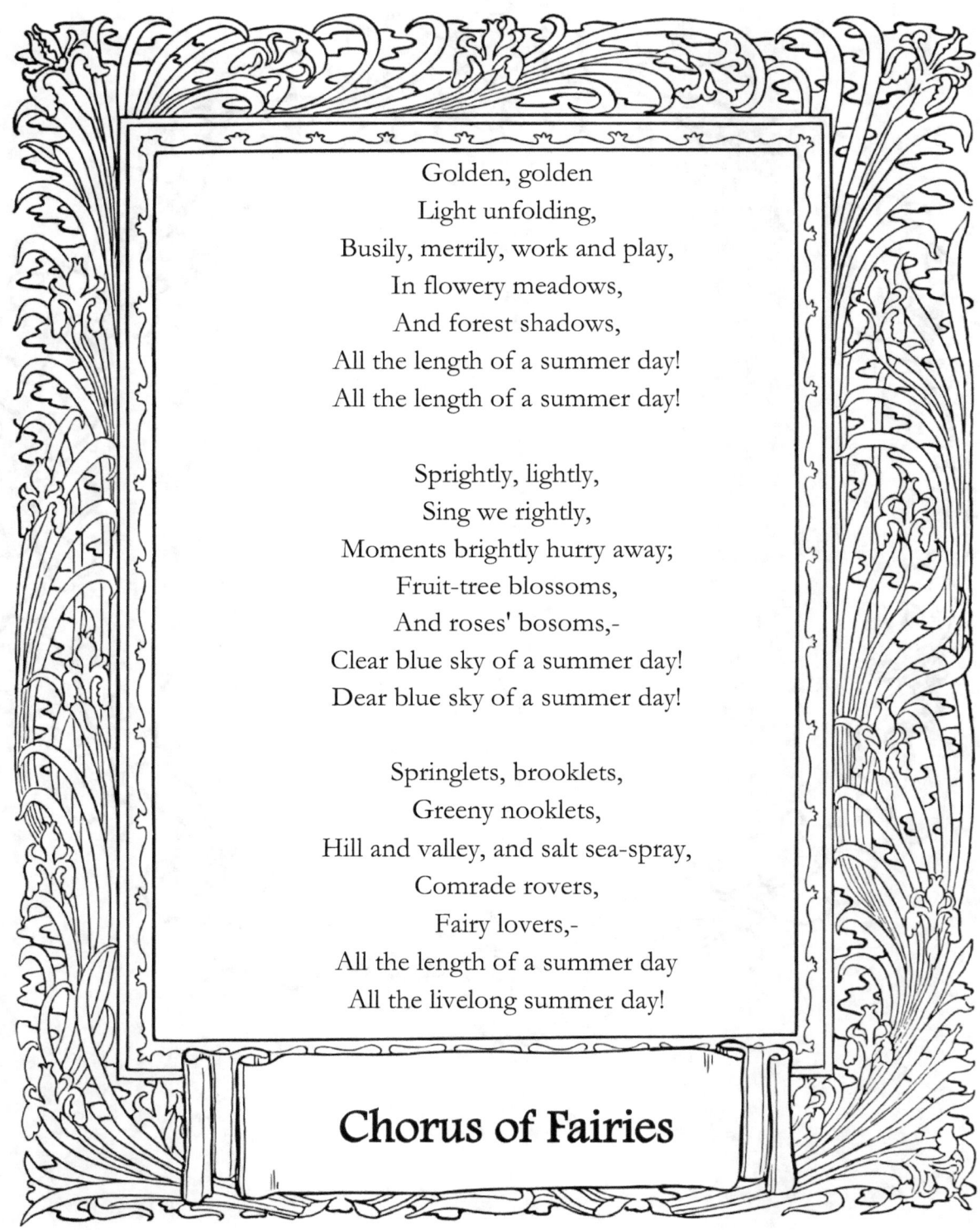

Golden, golden
Light unfolding,
Busily, merrily, work and play,
In flowery meadows,
And forest shadows,
All the length of a summer day!
All the length of a summer day!

Sprightly, lightly,
Sing we rightly,
Moments brightly hurry away;
Fruit-tree blossoms,
And roses' bosoms,-
Clear blue sky of a summer day!
Dear blue sky of a summer day!

Springlets, brooklets,
Greeny nooklets,
Hill and valley, and salt sea-spray,
Comrade rovers,
Fairy lovers,-
All the length of a summer day
All the livelong summer day!

Chorus of Fairies

SYNOPSIS

The poem describes a delightful summer day of fairies working and playing.

ENRICHMENT ACTIVITIES

1. **Recite Poem Information**
   Practice reciting the title of the poem and the name of the poet.

2. **Narrate the Poem**
   Verbally recount poem events in your own words.

3. **Color the Poem Frame**
   Color the frame surrounding the poem.

4. **Act Out the Poem**
   - Pretend to be a fairy frolicking through a field of flowers on a sunny day.
   - Stop to pick a flower and smell the delicious fragrance.

5. **Explore Rhyming**
   Find and recite the rhyming words in the poem.

VOCABULARY

Students Recite Words	Students Listen to the Definitions
unfolding	Open or spread out from a folded position.
sprightly	Lively and full of energy.
brooklet	A little spring (water).
nooklet	A little nook or corner.
comrade	A companion who shares one's activities.
rover	A person who spends their time wandering.

REVIEW QUESTIONS

1. What is the title of the poem?
2. What happens in the poem?
3. Where does the poem take place?
4. Who are the characters in the poem?
5. What does the poem teach the reader?

TRACEWORK AND/OR COPYWORK

Golden, golden

Light unfolding,

Busily, merrily, work and play.

DRAW THE POEM (Depict a fairy playing in a meadow.)

LESSON 17: "THE FAIRY SHOEMAKER" (EXCERPT) BY WILLIAM ALLINGHAM

FEATURED POEM

1. Little Cowboy, what have you heard,
Up on the lonely rath's green mound?
Only the plaintive yellow bird
Sighing in sultry fields around,

2. Chary, chary, chary, chee-ee!-
Only the grasshopper and the bee?-
Tip-tap, rip-rap,
Tick-a-tack-too!

3. Scarlet leather sewn together,
This will make a shoe.
Left, right, pull it tight;
Summer days are warm;
Underground in winter,
Laughing at the storm!"

4. Lay your ear close to the hill.
Do you not catch the tiny clamor,
Busy click of an Elfin hammer,
Voice of the Leprechaun singing shrill
As he merrily plies his trade?
He's a span
And a quarter in height.
Get him in sight, hold him tight,
And you're a made man!

5. I caught him at work one day, myself,
In the castle-ditch where foxglove grows,-
 wrinkled, wizen'd, and bearded Elf,
Spectacles stuck on his pointed nose,
Silver buckles to his hose,
Leather apron-shoe in his lap-
Rip-rap, tip-tap,
Tack-tack-too!

6. (A green cricket on my cap!
Away the moth flew!)
Buskins for a fairy prince,
Brogues for his son,-
Pay me well, pay me well,
When the job is done!"
The rogue was mine, beyond a doubt.

7. I stared at him, he stared at me;
"Servant, Sir!" "Humph!" says he,
And pull'd a snuff-box out.
He took a long pinch, look'd better pleased,
The queer little Leprechaun;
Offer'd the box with a whimsical grace,
Pouf! he flung the dust in my face,
And, while I sneezed,
Was gone!

SYNOPSIS

The narrator asks us whether we have heard the hammer of the Elfin shoemaker working up on the mound. The narrator advises if you capture the shoemaker you may use him to make yourself rich. The narrator saw the tricky elf once, but before he could act, the elf threw snuff in his face and disappeared.

ENRICHMENT ACTIVITIES

1. **Recite Poem Information**
   Practice reciting the title of the poem and the name of the poet.
2. **Narrate the Poem**
   Verbally recount poem events in your own words.
3. **Study the Poem Picture**
   Study the poem picture and describe how it relates to the poem.
4. **Can You Find It?**
   Find the following in the poem picture: Elf, hat, belt, and shoes.
5. **Explore Rhyming**
   Find and recite the rhyming words in the poem.

VOCABULARY

Students Recite Words	Students Listen to the Definitions
rath	The circular earthen residence of an ancient Irish chief.
plies	Works steadily at one's business or trade.
span	The width of a person's hand, as measured from the tip of the thumb to the tip of the little finger, when the fingers and thumb are spread out.
sup	Eat supper.
crock	An earthenware pot or jar.
miser	A person who hoards wealth and spends as little money as possible.
foxglove	A tall plant with erect spikes of flowers, typically pinkish-purple or white, shaped like the fingers of gloves.
hose	Stockings, socks, and tights.
buskin	A calf-high or knee-high boot of cloth or leather.
brogue	A strong outdoor shoe with ornamental perforated patterns in the leather.

ELEMENTARY POETRY VOLUME 2: POETRY OF FABLES, FAIRIES, AND FAUNA

REVIEW QUESTIONS

1. What is the title of the poem?
2. Where does the poem take place?
3. What happens in the poem?
4. Who are the characters in the poem?

TRACEWORK AND/OR COPYWORK

Chary, chary, chary, chee-eei-

Only the grasshopper and bee?

Tip-top, rip-rap,

Tick-a-tack-too!

DRAW THE POEM (Illustrate a shoemaker elf and his workshop.)

PART III: POETRY OF FAUNA
LESSON 18: "ROBIN REDBREAST" BY WILLIAM ALLINGHAM

FEATURED POEM

1. Goodbye, goodbye to Summer!
For Summer's nearly done;
The garden smiling faintly,
Cool breezes in the sun;
Our Thrushes now are silent,
Our Swallows flown away,-

2. But Robin's here, in coat of brown,
With ruddy breast-knot gay.
Robin, Robin Redbreast,
O Robin dear!
Robin singing sweetly
In the falling of the year.

3. Bright yellow, red, and orange,
The leaves come down in hosts;
The trees are Indian Princes,
But soon they'll turn to Ghosts;
The scanty pears and apples
Hang russet on the bough,

4. It's Autumn, Autumn, Autumn late,
'Twill soon be Winter now.
Robin, Robin Redbreast,
O Robin dear!
And welaway! my Robin,
For pinching times are near.

5. The fireside for the Cricket,
The wheatstack for the Mouse,
When trembling night-winds whistle
And moan all round the house;
The frosty ways like iron,
The branches plumed with snow,-

6. Alas! in Winter, dead and dark,
Where can poor Robin go?
Robin, Robin Redbreast,
O Robin dear,
And a crumb of bread for Robin,
His little heart to cheer.

SYNOPSIS

The poem narrator warns a robin that summer is ending and winter is near, describing the changes in weather, flora, and fauna accompanying the fall.

ENRICHMENT ACTIVITIES

1. **Recite Poem Information**
   Practice reciting the title of the poem and the name of the poet.
2. **Narrate the Poem**
   Verbally recount poem events in your own words.
3. **Study the Poem Pictures**
   Study the poem pictures and describe how they relate to the poem.
4. **Can You Find It?**
   Find the following in the poem pictures: Stem, leaf veins, beak, tail feathers, claws, and branch.
5. **Explore Rhyming**
   Find and recite the rhyming words in the poem.

VOCABULARY

Students Recite Words	Students Listen to the Definitions
thrushes	A songbird, typically having a brown back, spotted breast, and loud song.
swallows	A migratory swift-flying songbird with a forked tail and long pointed wings, feeding on insects in flight.
scanty	Small or insufficient in quantity or amount.
welaway	Alas; An expression of sadness or regret.
pinching times	The time to harvest or prune a plant.
plumed	Spread out in a shape resembling a feather

REVIEW QUESTIONS

1. What is the title of the poem?
2. What happens in the poem?
3. Who are the characters in the poem?
4. What does the poem teach the reader?

TRACEWORK AND/OR COPYWORK

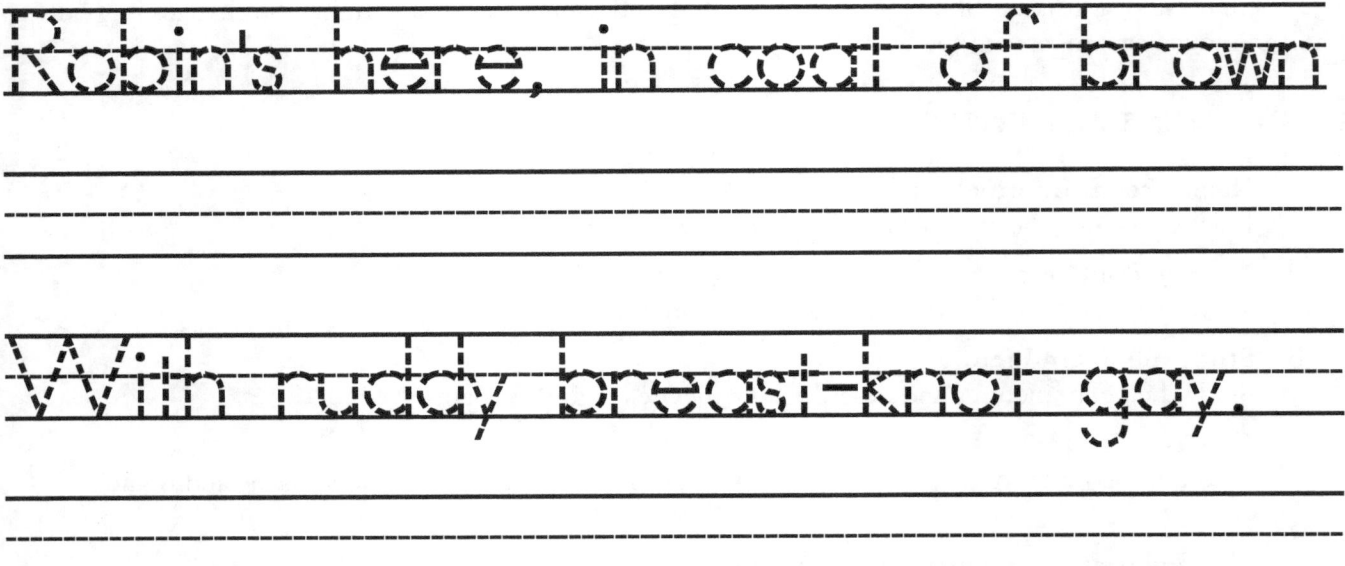

Robins here, in coat of brown

With ruddy breast-knot gay.

DRAW THE POEM (Color the autumn tree leaves red, yellow, orange, and/or brown. Add falling leaves in the air and on the ground surrounding the tree trunk.)

LESSON 19: "DREAMING" BY WILLIAM ALLINGHAM

FEATURED POEM

1. A strange little Dream
On a long star-beam
Ran down from the midnight skies,
To curly-hair'd Fred
Asleep in his bed,
With the lids on his merry blue eyes.

2. Under each lid
The thin Dream slid,
And spread to a picture inside,
A new World there,
Most strange and rare,
Tho' just by our garden-side.

3. Rivers and Rocks,
And a Treasure-Box,
And Floating in Air without wings,
And the Speaking Beast,
And a Royal Feast,
My chair beside the King's;

4. A Land of Flowers,
And of lofty Towers
Carved over in marble white
With living Shapes
Of Panthers and Apes
That gambol in ceaseless flight;

5. And a Cellar small
With its Cave in the Wall
Stretching many a mile underground!
And the Rope from the Moon!—
Fred woke too soon,
For its end could never be found.

SYNOPSIS

The poem describes a dream slipping down from the sky to slide under the eyelids of a boy. The poem then relates the fantastical dream experienced by the boy.

ELEMENTARY POETRY VOLUME 2: POETRY OF FABLES, FAIRIES, AND FAUNA

ENRICHMENT ACTIVITIES

1. **Recite Poem Information**
   Practice reciting the title of the poem and the name of the poet.

2. **Narrate the Poem**
   Verbally recount poem events in your own words.

3. **Study the Poem Picture**
   Study the poem picture and describe how it relates to the poem.

4. **Can You Find It?**
   Find the following in the poem picture: Someone sleeping, dream, woman, wheel, and spokes.

5. **Explore Rhyming**
   Find and recite the rhyming words in the poem.

VOCABULARY

Students Recite Words	Students Listen to the Definitions
royal	Having the status of a king or queen or a member of their family.
feast	A large meal, typically one in celebration of something.
lofty	Very high.
tower	A tall narrow building.
ape	A large primate that lacks a tail, including the gorilla, chimpanzees, orangutan, and gibbons.
gambol	Run or jump about playfully.
ceaseless	Never stopping, constant.
cellar	A room below ground level in a house.

REVIEW QUESTIONS

1. What is the title of the poem?

2. Where does the poem take place?

3. What happens in the poem?

4. Who are the characters in the poem?

5. What does the poem teach the reader?

TRACEWORK AND/OR COPYWORK

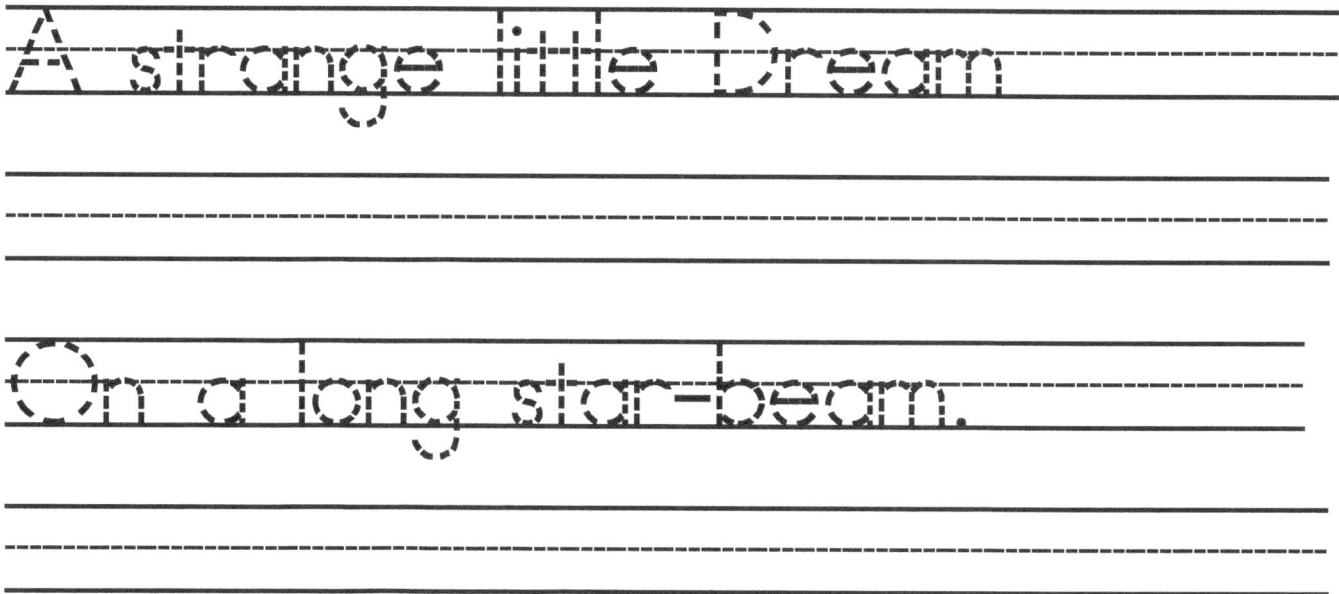

A strange little Dream
On a long star-beam.

DRAW THE POEM (Depict a dream you once experienced.)

ELEMENTARY POETRY VOLUME 2: POETRY OF FABLES, FAIRIES, AND FAUNA

LESSON 20: "I LOVE YOU, DEAR"
BY WILLIAM ALLINGHAM

FEATURED POEM

I love you, Dear, I love you, Dear,
You can't think how I love you, Dear!
Supposing I
Were a Butterfly,
I'd waver around and above you, Dear.

A long way off I spied you, Dear,
No bonnet or hat could hide you, Dear,
If I were a Bird,
Believe my word,
I'd sing every day beside you, Dear.

When you're away I miss you, Dear,
And now you're here I'll kiss you, Dear,
And beg you will take
This flow'r for my sake,
And my love along with this, you Dear!

SYNOPSIS

The poem narrator expresses their deep love for another, perhaps a parent showing love for their child.

ENRICHMENT ACTIVITIES

1. **Recite Poem Information**
   Practice reciting the title of the poem and the name of the poet.

2. **Narrate the Poem**
   Verbally recount poem events in your own words.

3. **Study the Poem Pictures**
   Study the poem pictures and describe how they relate to the poem.

4. **Can You Find It?**
   Find the following in the poem pictures: Mother, apron, baby, diaper, heart, leaves, and vines.

5. **Explore Rhyming**
   Find and recite the rhyming words in the poem.

VOCABULARY

Students Recite Words	Students Listen to the Definitions
waver	Shake with a quivering motion.
spied	Discern or make out, especially by careful observation.
bonnet	A woman's or child's hat tied under the chin, typically with a brim framing the face.
beg	Ask someone earnestly or humbly for something.
flow'r	Contraction of flower.
sake	Out of consideration for or to help someone.

REVIEW QUESTIONS

1. What is the title of the poem?
2. What happens in the poem?
3. Who are the characters in the poem?
4. What does the poem teach the reader?

TRACEWORK AND/OR COPYWORK

Supposing I Were a Butterfly,

I'd waver around you, Dear.

DRAW THE POEM (Illustrate what love means to you.)

LESSON 21: "SEASONS" BY WILLIAM ALLINGHAM

FEATURED POEM

1. In Spring-time, the Forest,
In Summer, the Sea,
In Autumn, the Mountains,
In Winter,-ah me!

2. How gay, the old branches
A-swarm with new buds,
The primrose and bluebell
Fresh-blown in the woods,
All green things unfolding,
Where merry birds sing!
I love in the Woodlands
To wander in Spring.

3. What joy, when the Sea-waves,
In mirth and in might,
Spread purple in shadow,
Flash white into light!
The gale fills the sail,
And the gull flies away;
In crimson and gold
Sets the long Summer Day.

4. O pride! on the Mountains
To leave earth below;
The great slopes of heather,
One broad purple glow;
The loud-roaring torrent
Leaps, bound after bound,
To plains of gold Autumn,
With mist creeping round.

5. Ah, Wind, is it Winter?
Yes, Winter is here;
With snow on the meadow,
And ice on the mere.
The daylight is short,
But the firelight is long;
Our skating's good sport;
Then story and song.

6. In Spring-time, the Forest,
In Summer, the Sea,
In Autumn, the Mountains,-
And Winter has glee.

SYNOPSIS

The poem narrator describes what they cherish about each of the four seasons of spring, summer, autumn, and winter.

ENRICHMENT ACTIVITIES

1. **Recite Poem Information**
   Practice reciting the title of the poem and the name of the poet.

2. **Narrate the Poem**
   Verbally recount poem events in your own words.

3. **Study the Poem Pictures**
   Study the poem pictures and describe how they relate to the poem.

4. **Can You Find It?**
   Find the following in the poem pictures: Spring blooms, fall leaves, and bare winter branches.

5. **Explore Rhyming**
   Find and recite the rhyming words in the poem.

VOCABULARY

Students Recite Words	Students Listen to the Definitions
swarm	Move somewhere in large numbers.
mirth	Amusement, especially as expressed in laughter.
gale	A strong wind.
gull	A long-winged, web-footed seabird with a raucous call, typically having white plumage with a gray or black mantle.
crimson	Of a rich deep red color inclining to purple.
heather	A purple-flowered shrub that grows abundantly on moorland and heathland.
torrent	A strong and fast-moving stream of water or other liquid.

REVIEW QUESTIONS

1. What is the title of the poem?

2. What happens in the poem?

3. Who are the characters in the poem?

4. What does the poem teach the reader?

TRACEWORK AND/OR COPYWORK

All green things unfolding

Where merry birds sing!

DRAW THE POEM (Sketch your favorite season.)

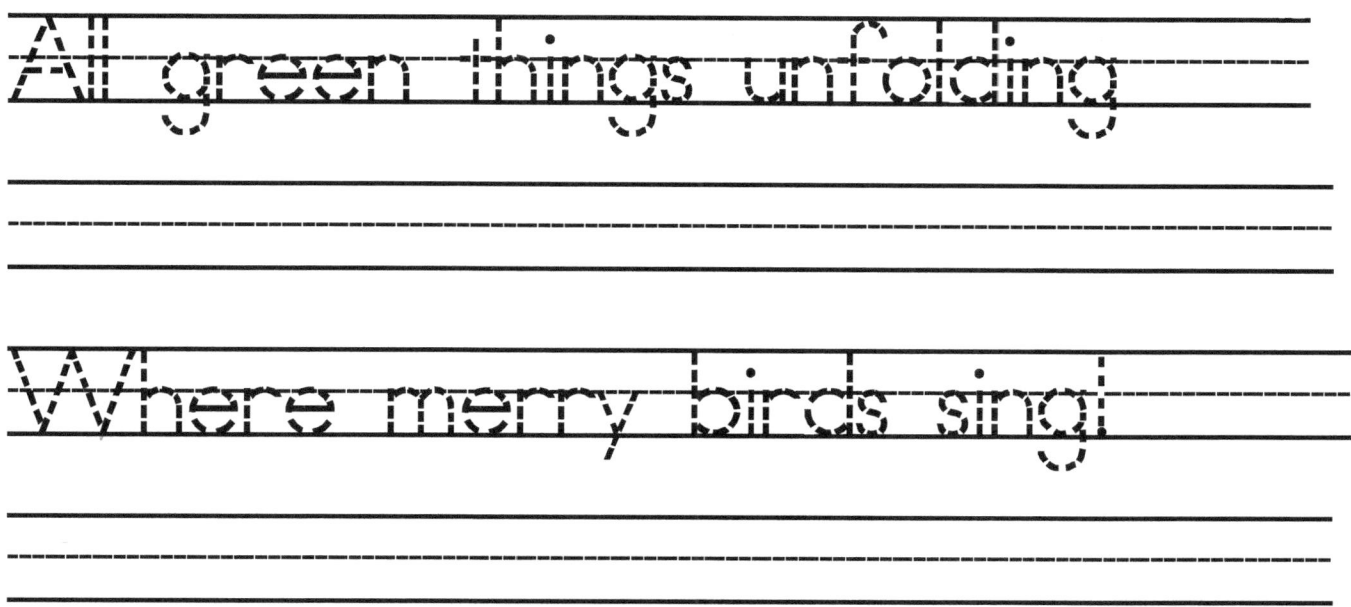

LESSON 22: "THE CAT AND THE DOG" BY WILLIAM ALLINGHAM

FEATURED POEM

1. There once lived a Man, a Cat, and a Dog,
And the Man built a house with stone and log.
"If you'll help to take care of this house with me,
One indoors, one out, your places must be."
Said both together, "Indoors I'll stay!"
And they argued the matter for half-a-day.

2. "Come, let us sing for it!" purrs the Cat;
"No!" barks the Dog, "I won't do that."
"Come, let us fight for it!" growls Bow-wow;
"Nay!" says Pussy, "mee-ow, mee-ow!"
"Well, let us race for it!"-said and done.
The course is mark'd out, and away they run.

3. Puss bounded off; the Dog ran fast;
Quickly was Puss overtaken and pass'd;
But a Beggar who under the hedge did lie
Struck the poor Dog as he gallop'd by
A blow with his staff, and lessen'd his pace
To a limp: so Pussy won the race.

4. The Beggar went on his way to beg;
Dog was cured of his limping leg;
And Cat keeps the inside of the house,
Watching it well from rat and mouse,
Dog keeps the outside, ever since then,
And always barks at beggar-men.

SYNOPSIS

A man tells a cat and dog that one may stay inside the house and the other must live outside. Both cat and dog want to live inside, so they race for it. During the race, a beggar man strikes the dog with a staff, causing the dog to lose the race. Thereafter, the dog must remain outside, barking resentfully at beggars ever since.

ENRICHMENT ACTIVITIES

1. **Recite Poem Information**
   Practice reciting the title of the poem and the name of the poet.
2. **Narrate the Poem**
   Verbally recount poem events in your own words.
3. **Study the Poem Picture**
   Study the poem picture and describe how it relates to the poem.
4. **Act Out the Poem**
   - Clear a room or go outdoors to hold foot races from one point to another.
   - Children act out winning, losing, and tying.
5. **Discuss the Poem**
   - Discuss whether you think the race between the dog and cat in the poem was fair.
   - Do you think the dog agrees with the old saying, "It's not whether you win or lose, it's how you play the game."
6. **Explore Rhyming**
   Find and recite the rhyming words in the poem.

VOCABULARY

Students Recite Words	Students Listen to the Definitions
race	A competition between runners, horses, vehicles, boats, etc., to see which is the fastest in covering a set course.
overtake	Catch up with and pass while traveling in the same direction.
hedge	A fence or boundary formed by closely growing bushes or shrubs.
blow	A powerful stroke with a hand, weapon, or hard object.
staff	A long stick used as a support when walking or climbing or as a weapon.
limp	To walk with difficulty, typically because of a damaged or stiff leg or foot.

REVIEW QUESTIONS

1. What is the title of the poem?
2. What happens in the poem?
3. Who are the characters in the poem?
4. What does the poem teach the reader?

TRACEWORK AND/OR COPYWORK

Cat keeps inside of the house

Watching it from rat and mouse.

Dog keeps outside, since then,

And always barks at beggar-men.

DRAW THE POEM (Color the cat and dog racing.)

LESSON 23: "THE BIRD"
BY WILLIAM ALLINGHAM

FEATURED POEM

1. "Birdie, Birdie, will you pet?
Summer-time is far away yet,
You'll have silken quilts and a velvet bed,
And a pillow of satin for your head!"

2. "I'd rather sleep in the ivy wall;
No rain comes through, tho' I hear it fall;
The sun peeps gay at dawn of day,
And I sing, and wing away, away!"

3. "O Birdie, Birdie, will you pet?
Diamond-stones and amber and jet
We'll string for a necklace fair and fine
To please this pretty bird of mine!"

The Cheerful Chickadee

4. "O thanks for diamonds, and thanks for jet,
But there is something daintier yet,-
A feather-necklace round and round,
That I wouldn't sell for a thousand pound!"

5. "O Birdie, Birdie, won't you pet?
We'll buy you a dish of silver fret,
A golden cup and an ivory seat,
And carpets soft beneath your feet!"

6. "Can running water be drunk from gold?
Can a silver dish the forest hold?
A rocking twig is the finest chair,
And the softest paths lie through the air,-
Good-bye, good-bye to my lady fair!"

The Charming Chaffinch

SYNOPSIS

A child tries to convince a bird to become her pet. The odd verses (1, 3, ...) are the child's arguments and the even verses are the bird's replies. In the end, the bird prefers freedom in the wild to a pampered life in a cage, for the "forest cannot be held within a silver dish."

ENRICHMENT ACTIVITIES

1. **Recite Poem Information**
   Practice reciting the title of the poem and the name of the poet.

2. **Narrate the Poem**
   Verbally recount poem events in your own words.

3. **Study the Poem Pictures**
   Study the poem pictures and describe how they relate to the poem.

4. **Can You Find It?**
   Find the following in the poem pictures: Chickadee, chaffinch, tail feathers, beaks, wings, and feet.

5. **Explore Rhyming**
   Find and recite the rhyming words in the poem.

6. **Discuss the Poem**
   If you were a bird, would you rather live with the child in a cage or out in the forest?
   - Living with the child, you would eat from a pretty silver dish and never be hungry or cold.
   - Living in the forest, you would be free to go where you pleased and do as you like.

VOCABULARY

Students Recite Words	Students Listen to the Definitions
silken	Made of silk or feeling like silk, a fine, soft cloth woven from silk fibers.
velvet	A closely woven fabric of silk, cotton, or nylon, that has a thick short pile on one side.
satin	A smooth, glossy fabric, typically of silk.
ivy	A woody evergreen Eurasian climbing plant, typically having shiny, dark green five-pointed leaves.
amber	A hard translucent fossilized resin produced by extinct coniferous trees of the Tertiary period, typically yellowish in color.
jet	A hard black semiprecious variety of lignite coal, capable of being carved and highly polished.
fret	To be constantly or visibly worried or anxious.

REVIEW QUESTIONS

1. What is the title of the poem?

2. What happens in the poem?

3. Who are the characters in the poem?

4. What does the poem teach the reader?

TRACEWORK AND/OR COPYWORK

Can water be drunk from gold?

Can silver dish the forest hold?

A rocking twig is the finest chair.

Softest paths lie through the air.

DRAW THE POEM (Depict yourself as a bird living in a forest. Which season is it? Are you singing, flying, building a nest, feeding your babies, etc.?)

The Forest Bird

LESSON 24: "WISHING"
BY WILLIAM ALLINGHAM

FEATURED POEM

1. Ring-ting! I wish I were a Primrose,
A bright yellow Primrose blowing in the Spring!
The stooping boughs above me,
The wandering bee to love me,
The fern and moss to creep across,
And the Elm-tree for our king!

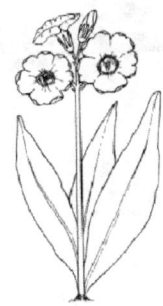

2. Nay-stay! I wish I were an Elm-tree,
A great lofty Elm-tree, with green leaves gay!
The winds would set them dancing,
The sun and moonshine glancing,
The Birds would house among the boughs,
And sweetly sing!

3. O-no! I wish I were a Robin,
A Robin or a little Wren, everywhere to go;
Through forest, field, or garden,
And ask no leave or pardon,
Till Winter comes with icy thumbs
To ruffle up our wing.

4. Well-tell! Where should I fly to,
Where go to sleep in the dark wood or dell?
Before a day was over,
Here comes the rover,
For Mother's kiss,-sweeter this
Than any other thing!

SYNOPSIS

The narrator wishes they were a primrose, an elm tree, and finally a robin, but worries about sleeping accommodations at night and missing the sweetness of their mother's kiss.

ENRICHMENT ACTIVITIES

1. **Recite Poem Information**
   Practice reciting the title of the poem and the name of the poet.
2. **Narrate the Poem**
   Verbally recount poem events in your own words.
3. **Study the Poem Pictures**
   Study the poem pictures and describe how they relate to the poem.
4. **Can You Find It?**
   Find the following in the poem pictures: Primrose, elm tree, robin, and rovers.
5. **Act Out the Poem**
   Pretend to be a blooming primrose, a lofty elm waving in the breeze, and a hopping robin.
6. **Explore Rhyming**
   Find and recite the rhyming words in the poem.

VOCABULARY

Students Recite Words	Students Listen to the Definitions
primrose	A plant that produces pale yellow flowers in the early spring.
fern	A flowerless plant that has feathery or leafy fronds.
moss	A small flowerless green plant that lacks true roots.
ruffle	Disorder or disarrange hair or feathers.
dell	A small valley, usually among trees.

REVIEW QUESTIONS

1. What is the title of the poem?
2. What happens in the poem?
3. Who are the characters in the poem?
4. What does the poem teach the reader?

TRACEWORK AND/OR COPYWORK

Well-tell Where should I fly to,

Where to sleep in the dark dell?

DRAW THE POEM (Sketch yourself playing in the woods.)

LESSON 25: "I SAW A LITTLE BIRDIE FLY" BY WILLIAM ALLINGHAM

FEATURED POEM

I saw a little Birdie fly,
Merrily piping came he;
"Whom d'ye sing to, Bird?" said I;
"Sing?-I sing to Amy!"

"Very sweet you sing," I said;
"Then," quoth he, "to pay me,
Give one little crumb of bread,
A little smile from Amy."

"Just," he sings, "one little smile;
O, a frown would slay me!
Thanks, and now I'm gone awhile,-
Fare-you-well, dear Amy!"

SYNOPSIS

The poem narrator spots a singing bird, and the bird reveals it sings to Amy. The bird asks for payment for its song, a crumb and a smile from Amy.

ENRICHMENT ACTIVITIES

1. **Recite Poem Information**
   Practice reciting the title of the poem and the name of the poet.

2. **Narrate the Poem**
   Verbally recount poem events in your own words.

3. **Study the Poem Picture**
   Study the poem picture and describe how it relates to the poem.

4. **Can You Find It?**
   Find the following in the poem picture: Birds, nest, vines, leaves, and flowers.

5. **Explore Rhyming**
   Find and recite the rhyming words in the poem.

VOCABULARY

Students Recite Words	Students Listen to the Definitions
piping	A bird singing in a high or shrill voice.
quoth	Another word for "said."
slay	Kill a person or animal in a violent way.
fare	Happen or turn out.

REVIEW QUESTIONS

1. What is the title of the poem?

2. Where does the poem take place?

3. What happens in the poem?

4. Who are the characters in the poem?

TRACEWORK AND/OR COPYWORK

I saw a little Birdie fly,

Merrily piping came he.

DRAW THE POEM (Imagine you have a pet bird, and color it on the sign.)

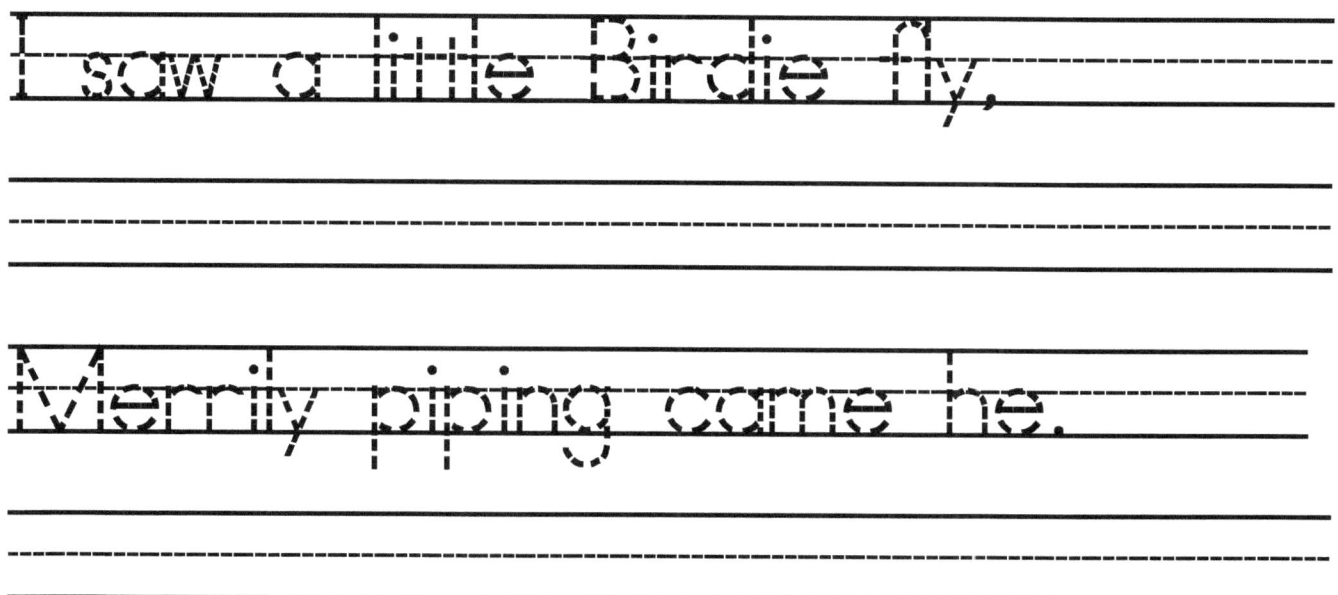

LESSON 26: "A MOUNTAIN ROUND" BY WILLIAM ALLINGHAM

FEATURED POEM

Take hands, merry neighbors, for dancing the round!

Moonlight is fair and delicious the air;

From valley to valley our music shall sound,

And startle the wolf in his lair.

From summits of snow to the forest below,

Let vulture and crow hear the echoes, O-ho! (O-ho!)

While shadow on meadow in dancing the round

Goes whirligig, pair after pair!

SYNOPSIS

The narrator calls for their neighbors to take hands and dance the round under the moonlight.

ENRICHMENT ACTIVITIES

1. **Recite Poem Information**
   Practice reciting the title of the poem and the name of the poet.

2. **Narrate the Poem**
   Verbally recount poem events in your own words.

3. **Study the Poem Picture**
   Study the poem picture and describe how it relates to the poem.

4. **Can You Find It?**
   Find the following in the poem picture: Ladies, mountains, clouds, bushes, valley, cloaks, and bird.

5. **Act Out the Poem**
   Find an open, safe space to dance the round while reciting the poem.

6. **Explore Rhyming**
   Find and recite the rhyming words in the poem.

VOCABULARY

Students Recite Words	Students Listen to the Definitions
round	A folk dance in which the dancers form one large circle.
fair	Beautiful, of a pleasing appearance, with a pure and fresh quality.
valley	An elongated depression between hills or mountains.
lair	A wild animal's resting place.
summit	The highest point of a hill or mountain.
whirligig	A toy that spins around, for example, a top or a pinwheel.

REVIEW QUESTIONS

1. What is the title of the poem?
2. Where does the poem take place?
3. What happens in the poem?
4. Who are the characters in the poem?
5. What does the poem teach the reader?

TRACEWORK AND/OR COPYWORK

Take hands, merry neighbors

for dancing the round!

DRAW THE POEM (Depict your family or friends dancing the round.)

LESSON 27: "BIRDS' NAMES" BY WILLIAM ALLINGHAM

FEATURED POEM

1. Of Creatures with Feathers, come let us see
Which have names like you and me.
Hook-nosed Poll, that thinks herself pretty,
Everyone knows, of all birds most witty.

2. Friendly Daw, in suit of gray,
Ask him his name, and "Jack!" he'll say.
Pert Philip Sparrow hopping you meet,
"Philip! Philip!"-in garden and street.

3. Bold Robin Redbreast perches near,
And sings his best in the fall of the year.
Grave Madge Owlet shuns the light,
And shouts "hoo! hoo!" in the woods at night.

4. Nightingale sweet, that May loves well,
Old Poets have call'd her Philomel,
But Philomelos, he sings best,
While she sits listening in her nest.

5. Darting Martin!-tell me why
They call you Martin, I know not, I;
Martin the black, under cottage eaves,
Martin the small, in sandy caves.

6. Merry Willy Wagtail, what runs he takes!
Wherever he stops, his tail he shakes.
Head and tail little Jenny Wren perks,
As in and out of the hedge she jerks.

7. Brisk Tom Tit, the lover of trees,
Picks-off every fly and grub he sees.
Mag, the cunning chattering Pie,
Builds her home in a tree-top high,-
Mag, you're a terrible thief, O fie!

8. Tom and Philip and Jenny and Polly,
Madge and Martin and Robin and Willy,
Philomelos and friendly Jack,-
Mag the rogue, half-white, half-black,

9. Stole an egg from every Bird;
Such an uproar was never heard;
All of them flew upon Mag together,
And pluck'd her naked of every feather.
"You're not a Bird!" they told her then,
"You may go away and live among men!"

SYNOPSIS

The poem describes the characteristics and appearance of various birds. When Mag steals their eggs, they attack her and pluck her of all her feathers.

ENRICHMENT ACTIVITIES

1. **Recite Poem Information**
   Practice reciting the title of the poem and the name of the poet.

2. **Narrate the Poem**
   Verbally recount poem events in your own words.

3. **Study the Poem Picture**
   Study the poem picture and describe how it relates to the poem.

4. **Act Out the Poem**
   Pretend to be Mag, sneaking into another bird's nest and stealing an egg.

5. **Explore Rhyming**
   Find and recite the rhyming words in the poem.

VOCABULARY

Students Recite Words	Students Listen to the Definitions
Philomel	Princess of Athens in Greek mythology who turns into a nightingale.
Philomelos	The song thrush.
grub	The larva of an insect.
cunning	Having or showing skill in achieving one's ends by deceit or evasion.
chattering	Make a series of quick high-pitched sounds.
fie	Used to express disgust or outrage.
rogue	A dishonest or unprincipled man.

REVIEW QUESTIONS

1. What is the title of the poem?

2. What happens in the poem?

3. Who are the characters in the poem?

4. What does the Mag do that upsets the other birds?

5. How do the birds get revenge on Mag?

TRACEWORK AND/OR COPYWORK

They flew on Mag together,

And pluck'd her of every feather.

DRAW THE POEM (Depict the birds plucking Mag's feathers off.)

LESSON 28: "NICK SPENCE"
BY WILLIAM ALLINGHAM

FEATURED POEM

Nick Spence, Nick Spence,
Sold the Cow for sixpence!
When his Master scolded him,
Nicky didn't care.
Put him in the farmyard,
The stableyard, the stackyard,
Send him to the pigsty,
And Johnny to the fair!

SYNOPSIS

Nick Spence sells his master's cow for far too little money. When Nick Spence feels no remorse, the poem narrator recommends punishing him by sending him to work on the farm instead of to the fair.

ENRICHMENT ACTIVITIES

1. **Recite Poem Information**
   Practice reciting the title of the poem and the name of the poet.

2. **Narrate the Poem**
   Verbally recount poem events in your own words.

3. **Study the Poem Picture**
   Study the poem picture and describe how it relates to the poem.

4. **Can You Find It?**
   Find the following in the poem picture: Farm house, barn, crops, cows, horses, pigs, and sheep.

5. **Act Out the Poem**
   - Pretend to be Nick Spence working extra time in the farmyard as a punishment.
   - Watch with disappoint as Johnny leaves without you for the fair.

6. **Explore Rhyming**
   Find and recite the rhyming words in the poem.

VOCABULARY

Students Recite Words	Students Listen to the Definitions
sixpence	A British coin worth six old pence, withdrawn in 1980.
scold	Admonish angrily.
stableyard	A yard or enclosure attached to horses' stables.
stackyard	A yard or enclosure for stacks of straw, hay, or grain.
pigsty	A pen for pigs.

REVIEW QUESTIONS

1. What is the title of the poem?
2. What happens in the poem?
3. Where does the poem take place?
4. Who are the characters in the poem?
5. What does the poem teach the reader?

ELEMENTARY POETRY VOLUME 2: POETRY OF FABLES, FAIRIES, AND FAUNA

TRACEWORK AND/OR COPYWORK

Nick Spence, Nick Spence,

Said the Cow for sixpence!

DRAW THE POEM (Illustrate Nick Spence being punished.)

LESSON 29: "RIDING" BY WILLIAM ALLINGHAM

FEATURED POEM

1. His Lordship's Steed
Of a noble breed
Is trotting it fleetly, fleetly,
Her Ladyship's pony,
Sleek and bonny,
Cantering neatly, neatly.

2. How shall they pass
The Turf-Cadger's Ass,
Creels and all, creels and all?
Man on him bumping,
Shouting and thumping,
Heels and all, heels and all!

3. Lane is not wide,
A hedge on each side,
The Ass is beginning to bray;
"Now," says my Lord,
With an angry word,
"Fellow, get out of the way!"

4. "Ha!" says the Cadger,
As bold as a badger,
"This way is my way too!"
Says the Lady mild,
And sweetly smiled,
"My Friend, that's perfectly true."

5. The Cadger look'd round,
Then jump'd to the ground,
And into the hedge pull'd Neddy.
"O thank you!" says she,
"Ax pardon!" says he,
And touch'd his old hat to the Lady.

6. His Lordship's Steed
Of a noble breed
Went trotting it fleetly, fleetly,
Her Ladyship's pony,
Sleek and bonny
Cantering neatly, neatly.

7. The Cadger he rode
As well as he could,
Heels and all, heels and all,
Jolting and bumping,
Shouting and thumping,
Creels and all, creels and all.

SYNOPSIS

A lady and a lord riding horseback encounter a poor man riding a donkey. The lord angrily orders the poor man out of their way, and the man refuses. When the lady treats the poor man kindly, he moves off to the side and tips his hat politely.

ENRICHMENT ACTIVITIES

1. **Recite Poem Information**
    Practice reciting the title of the poem and the name of the poet.
2. **Narrate the Poem**
    Verbally recount poem events in your own words.
3. **Study the Poem Picture**
    Study the poem picture and describe how it relates to the poem.
4. **Discuss the Poem**
    How does the old proverb, "You can catch more flies with honey than vinegar," apply to the poem?
5. **Explore Rhyming**
    Find and recite the rhyming words in the poem.

VOCABULARY

Students Recite Words	Students Listen to the Definitions
steed	A horse being ridden or available for riding.
noble	Of imposing or magnificent size or appearance.
breed	Animals or plants within a species having a distinctive appearance and typically having been developed by deliberate selection.
fleet	Fast and nimble in movement.
bonny	Attractive or beautiful.
canter	A three-beat gait of a horse between a trot and a gallop.
turf	Grass and the surface layer of earth held together by its roots.
cadger	Beggar.
badger	A heavily built omnivorous nocturnal mammal of the weasel family, typically having a gray and black coat.
ax	Slang for "ask."
creel	A wicker basket for carrying fish.

REVIEW QUESTIONS

1. What is the title of the poem?
2. What happens in the poem?
3. Who are the characters in the poem?
4. What does the poem teach the reader?

TRACEWORK AND/OR COPYWORK

"Now," says my Lord,

With an angry word,

"Fellow, get out of the way!"

DRAW THE POEM (Complete the outline of the horse. Add a scene from the poem around the horse.)

LESSON 30: "TOM CRICKET"
BY WILLIAM ALLINGHAM

FEATURED POEM

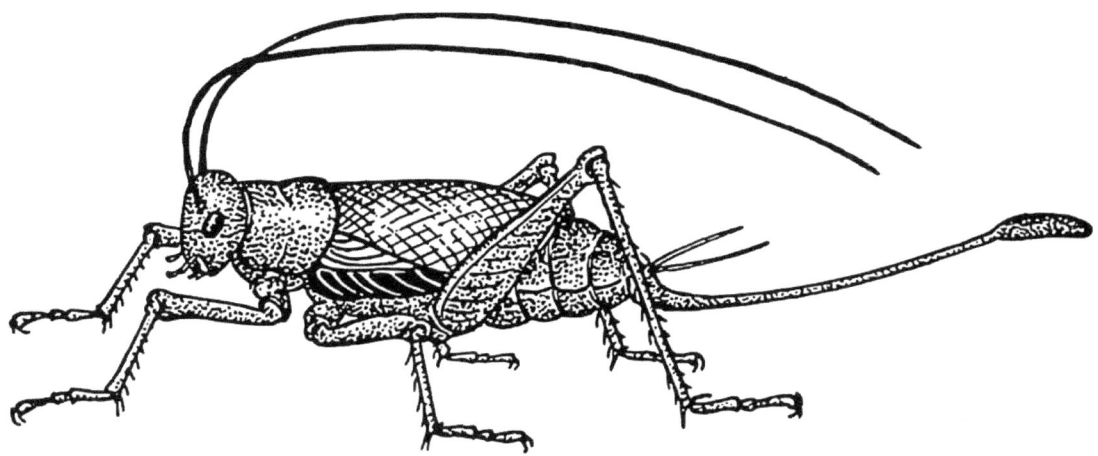

1. Tom Cricket he sat in his hole in the wall,
Close to the kitchen fire,
Up and down ran the Cockroaches all,
Red coats and black coats, great and small;
"Ho, Tom! our hearts are set on a ball,
And your music we desire!"

2. Tom sat in his hole, his horns hung out,
He play'd away on his fiddle;
The Cockroaches danced in a rabble rout,
Scrambling and scurrying all about,
Tho' they had their own steps and figures no doubt,
Hands across, and down the middle.

3. Till, "Stay!" says a Fat One,-"We're no Elves,
To dance all night without stopping!
Now for supper!" They help'd themselves,
For the servants were gone to bed; on shelves
And tables they quested by tens and twelves,
And quick to the floor kept dropping.

4. As a Cockroach ran by, says Tom Cricket to him,
"Fetch me up a piece of potato,
Good Sir!-to mix in the crowd I'm too slim."
Says Jack Cockroach, "I see you are proud and prim;
To eat alone is merely your whim,-
Which I never will give way to!"

5. "Come down," says he, "and look out for your share!"
"I won't do that," says Tom Cricket.
And when for another dance they care,
And call upon Tom for a lively air,
They find he has drawn himself back in his lair.
"How shameful," they cry, "How wicked!"

6. "Let's fill up the mouth of his cave with soot,
Because he's behaved so badly!"
They ran up and down the wall to do't;
But ere half-done-a dreadful salute!
In came the Cook, and the Scullion to boot,
And off they all scampered madly.

SYNOPSIS

Tom Cricket plays for some dancing cockroaches until they refuse to bring him food. When he stops playing, the cockroaches want revenge, but the cook and the scullion interrupt their plot.

ENRICHMENT ACTIVITIES

1. **Recite Poem Information**
   Practice reciting the title of the poem and the name of the poet.
2. **Narrate the Poem**
   Verbally recount poem events in your own words.
3. **Study the Poem Picture**
   Study the poem picture and describe how it relates to the poem.
4. **Explore Rhyming**
   Find and recite the rhyming words in the poem.

VOCABULARY

Students Recite Words	Students Listen to the Definitions
cricket	An insect related to the grasshoppers. The male produces a characteristic rhythmical chirping sound.
cockroach	A beetlelike insect with long antennae and legs.
rabble	A disorderly crowd.
rout	An assembly of people who have made a move toward committing an illegal act that would constitute an offense of riot
servant	A person who performs duties for others.
quested	Sought out.
prim	Stiffly formal and respectable.
soot	A black powdery or flaky substance produced by the incomplete burning of wood or other organic matter.
ere	Before in time.
salute	A gesture of respect or recognition.
scullion	A servant assigned the lowliest kitchen tasks such as scrubbing dishes.

REVIEW QUESTIONS

1. What is the title of the poem?
2. What happens in the poem?
3. Who are the characters in the poem?
4. What does the poem teach the reader?

TRACEWORK AND/OR COPYWORK

Tom Cricket sat in his hole

in the wall,

Close to the kitchen fire.

DRAW THE POEM (Depict Tom Cricket playing for the Cockroaches.)

LESSON 31: "LET DOGS DELIGHT TO BARK AND BITE" BY ISAAC WATTS

FEATURED POEM

Let dogs delight to bark and bite,
For God hath made them so;
Let bears and lions growl and fight,
For 'tis their nature too.

But, children, you should never let
Such angry passions rise;
Your little hands were never made
To tear each other's eyes.

SYNOPSIS

The poem advises children they were not meant to bark, bite, growl, and fight like dogs, bears, and lions. Humanity can rise above base instincts and be civilized with one another.

ENRICHMENT ACTIVITIES

1. **Recite Poem Information**
   Practice reciting the title of the poem and the name of the poet.

2. **Narrate the Poem**
   Verbally recount poem events in your own words.

3. **Study the Poem Picture**
   Study the poem picture and describe how it relates to the poem.

4. **Can You Find It?**
   - Find the following in the poem picture: Dogs, flowers, leaves, and vines.
   - How many dogs can you find?

5. **Explore Rhyming**
   Find and recite the rhyming words in the poem.

VOCABULARY

Students Recite Words	Students Listen to the Definitions
delight	Please someone greatly.
nature	The basic or inherent features of something.
passion	Strong and barely controllable emotion.
tear	Pull or rip apart.

REVIEW QUESTIONS

1. What is the title of the poem?

2. What happens in the poem?

3. Who are the characters in the poem?

4. What does the poem teach the reader?

TRACEWORK AND/OR COPYWORK

Children, you should never let

Such angry passions rise.

DRAW THE POEM (Color children playing peacefully in the picture frame.)

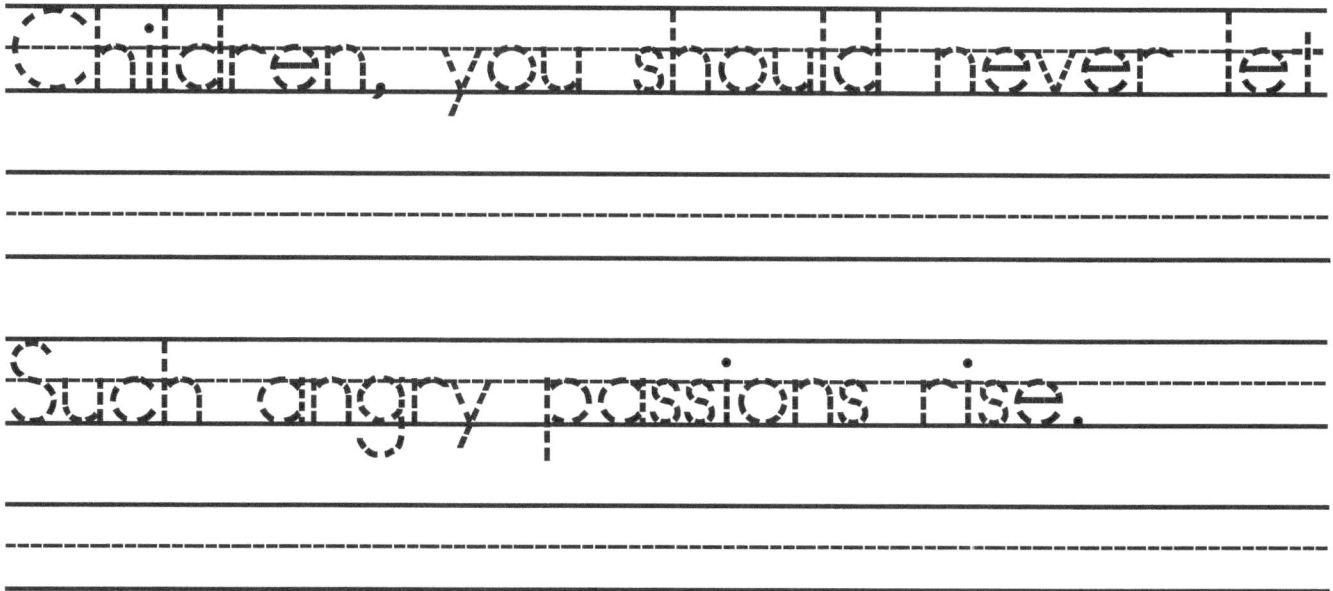

LESSON 32: "THE OWL & THE PUSSY CAT" BY EDWARD LEAR

FEATURED POEM

I. The Owl and the Pussy Cat went to sea

In a beautiful pea-green boat;

They took some honey, and plenty of money

Wrapped up in a five-pound note.

The Owl looked up to the moon above,

And sang to a small guitar,

"O lovely Pussy! O Pussy, my love!

What a beautiful Pussy you are,-

You are,

What a beautiful Pussy you are!"

II. Pussy said to the Owl, "You elegant fowl!

How wonderful sweet you sing!

Oh, let us be married,-too long we have tarried,-

But what shall we do for a ring?"

They sailed away for a year and a day

To the land where the Bong-tree grows,

And there in a wood a piggy-wig stood

With a ring in the end of his nose,-

His nose,

With a ring in the end of his nose.

III. "Dear Pig, are you willing to sell for one shilling

Your ring?" Said the piggy, "I will."

So they took it away, and were married next day

By the turkey who lives on the hill.

They dined upon mince and slices of quince,

Which they ate with a runcible spoon,

And hand in hand on the edge of the sand

They danced by the light of the moon,-

The moon,

They danced by the light of the moon.

SYNOPSIS

The Owl and the Pussy Cat sail on the sea, buy a ring from a piggy, get married, and dance in the light of the moon.

ENRICHMENT ACTIVITIES

1. **Recite Poem Information**
   Practice reciting the title of the poem and the name of the poet.
2. **Narrate the Poem**
   Verbally recount poem events in your own words.
3. **Study the Poem Pictures**
   Study the poem pictures and describe how they relate to the poem.
4. **Can You Find It?**
   Find the following in the poem pictures: Kitty, owl, piggy, ring, boat, honey, guitar, sea, and moon.
5. **Explore Rhyming**
   Find and recite the rhyming words in the poem.

VOCABULARY

Students Recite Words	Students Listen to the Definitions
note (five-pound)	Paper money.
fowl	A bird kept for its meat and its eggs including turkeys, geese, and ducks.
tarried	Stayed longer than intended.
bong-tree	A tropical evergreen tree.
shilling	A former British coin.
mince	Abbreviation for mincemeat - which refers to finely chopped meat or a mixture of currants, raisins, sugar, apples, candied citrus peel, spices, and suet, typically baked in a pie.
quince	A hard, acidic, pear-shaped fruit.
runcible	A nonsense word invented by the poet. Modern dictionaries define a "runcible spoon" as a fork with three curved tines.

REVIEW QUESTIONS

1. What is the title of the poem?

2. What happens in the poem?

3. Where does the poem take place?

4. Who are the characters in the poem?

TRACEWORK AND/OR COPYWORK

DRAW THE POEM (Sketch the Owl and the Pussy Cat marrying.)

LESSON 33: "A CHRYSALIS"
BY MARY EMILY BRADLEY

FEATURED POEM

1. My little Mädchen found one day
A curious something in her play,
That was not fruit, nor flower, nor seed;
It was not anything that grew,
Or crept, or climbed, or swam, or flew;
Had neither legs nor wings, indeed;
And yet she was not sure, she said,
Whether it was alive or dead.

2. She brought it in her tiny hand
To see if I would understand,
And wondered when I made reply,
"You've found a baby butterfly."
"A butterfly is not like this,"
With doubtful look she answered me.
So then I told her what would be
Someday within the chrysalis:
How, slowly, in the dull brown thing
Now still as death, a spotted wing,
And then another, would unfold,
Till from the empty shell would fly
A pretty creature, by and by,
All radiant in blue and gold.

3. "And will it, truly?" questioned she-
Her laughing lips and eager eyes
All in a sparkle of surprise-
"And shall your little Mädchen see?"
"She shall!" I said. How could I tell
That ere the worm within its shell
Its gauzy, splendid wings had spread,
My little Mädchen would be dead?

4. Today the butterfly has flown,-
She was not here to see it fly,-
And sorrowing I wonder why
The empty shell is mine alone.
Perhaps the secret lies in this:
I too had found a chrysalis,
And Death that robbed me of delight
Was but the radiant creature's flight!

SYNOPSIS

A little girl finds a chrysalis and the narrator explains a beautiful butterfly will emerge. The little girl dies before the butterfly emerges. When the butterfly sheds its cocoon and flies away, the narrator ponders that like the butterfly, the little girl may have shed her mortal shell to become something even more beautiful.

ENRICHMENT ACTIVITIES

1. **Recite Poem Information**
   Practice reciting the title of the poem and the name of the poet.

2. **Narrate the Poem**
   Verbally recount poem events in your own words.

3. **Study the Poem Pictures**
   Study the poem pictures and describe how they relate to the poem.

4. **Can You Find It?**
   Find the following in the poem pictures: Chrysalis, cocoon, butterfly, wings, and antennae.

5. **Explore Rhyming**
   Find and recite the rhyming words in the poem.

VOCABULARY

Students Recite Words	Students Listen to the Definitions
mädchen	Girl.
doubtful	Feeling uncertain about something.
chrysalis	Baby butterfly or moth that is enclosed in a hard shell.
shell	A hard protective outer case.
gauzy	Thin and allowing light, but not detailed images, to pass through.
sorrowing	Feeling or displaying deep distress.

REVIEW QUESTIONS

1. What is the title of the poem?
2. What happens in the poem?
3. Where does the poem take place?
4. Who are the characters in the poem?
5. What does the poem teach the reader?

TRACEWORK AND/OR COPYWORK

Then I told her what would be

Someday within the chrysalis.

DRAW THE POEM (Illustrate a butterfly emerging from a chrysalis.)

LESSON 34: "THE RAVEN" v. 1-6
BY EDGAR ALLAN POE

FEATURED POEM

1. Once upon a midnight dreary, while I pondered, weak and weary,

Over many a quaint and curious volume of forgotten lore-

While I nodded, nearly napping, suddenly there came a tapping,

As of someone gently rapping, rapping at my chamber door.

"'Tis some visitor," I muttered, "tapping at my chamber door-

Only this, and nothing more."

2. Ah! distinctly I remember, it was in the bleak December,

And each separate dying ember wrought its ghost upon the floor;

Eagerly I wished the morrow; vainly I had sought to borrow

From my books surcease of sorrow-sorrow for the lost Lenore-

For the rare and radiant maiden whom the angels name Lenore-

Nameless here for evermore.

3. And the silken, sad, uncertain rustling of each purple curtain

Thrilled me-filled me with fantastic terrors never felt before;

So that now, to still the beating of my heart, I stood repeating,

"'Tis some visitor entreating entrance at my chamber door-

Some late visitor entreating entrance at my chamber door:

This it is, and nothing more."

4. Presently my soul grew stronger; hesitating then no longer,

"Sir," said I, "or madam, truly your forgiveness I implore;

But the fact is, I was napping, and so gently you came rapping,

And so faintly you came tapping, tapping at my chamber door,

That I scarce was sure I heard you"-here I opened wide the door;-

Darkness there, and nothing more.

5. Deep into that darkness peering, long I stood there, wondering, fearing,

Doubting, dreaming dreams no mortal ever dared to dream before;

But the silence was unbroken, and the stillness gave no token,

And the only word there spoken was the whispered word, "Lenore!"

This I whispered, and an echo murmured back the word, "Lenore!"

Merely this, and nothing more.

6. Back into my chamber turning, all my soul within me burning,

Soon again I heard a rapping, something louder than before:

"Surely," said I, "surely that is something at my window lattice;

Let me see, then, what thereat is, and this mystery explore-

Let my heart be still a moment, and this mystery explore.

'Tis the wind, and nothing more."

SYNOPSIS

The narrator hears a tapping at his door. He feels nervous, but assures himself it is no more than a visitor knocking. He opens the door, but no one is there. All he hears is a whisper of the word, "Lenore." He returns to his chamber and the tapping starts again, even louder. He tells himself it is only the wind at his window.

ENRICHMENT ACTIVITIES

1. **Recite Poem Information**
   Practice reciting the title of the poem and the name of the poet.
2. **Narrate the Poem**
   Verbally recount poem events in your own words.
3. **Study the Poem Pictures**
   Study the poem pictures and describe how they relate to the poem.
4. **Can You Find It?**
   - Find the following in the first poem picture:
     - The Poem Narrator
     - Hiding Spirits
     - Staircase
     - Robe
     - Armchair
     - Framed Pictures
   - Find the following in the second poem picture:
     - The Poem Narrator
     - Sneaking Spirits
     - Window
     - Branches
     - Curtains
     - Shutters
5. **Explore Rhyming**
   Find and recite the rhyming words in the poem.

VOCABULARY

Students Recite Words	Students Listen to the Definitions
lore	A body of traditions and knowledge on a subject or held by a particular group, typically passed from person to person by word of mouth.
chamber	A private room, typically a bedroom.
ember	A small piece of burning or glowing coal or wood in a dying fire.
surcease	Cease, bring or come to an end.
entreating	Ask someone earnestly or anxiously to do something.

Students Recite Words	Students Listen to the Definitions
mortal	Of a living human being, often in contrast to a divine being, that is subject to death.
lattice	A structure consisting of strips of wood or metal crossed and fastened together with square or diamond-shaped spaces left between, used typically as a screen or fence or as a support for climbing plants.

REVIEW QUESTIONS

1. What is the title of the poem?
2. What happens in these verses of the poem?
3. Where does the poem take place?
4. Who are the characters in the poem?

TRACEWORK AND/OR COPYWORK

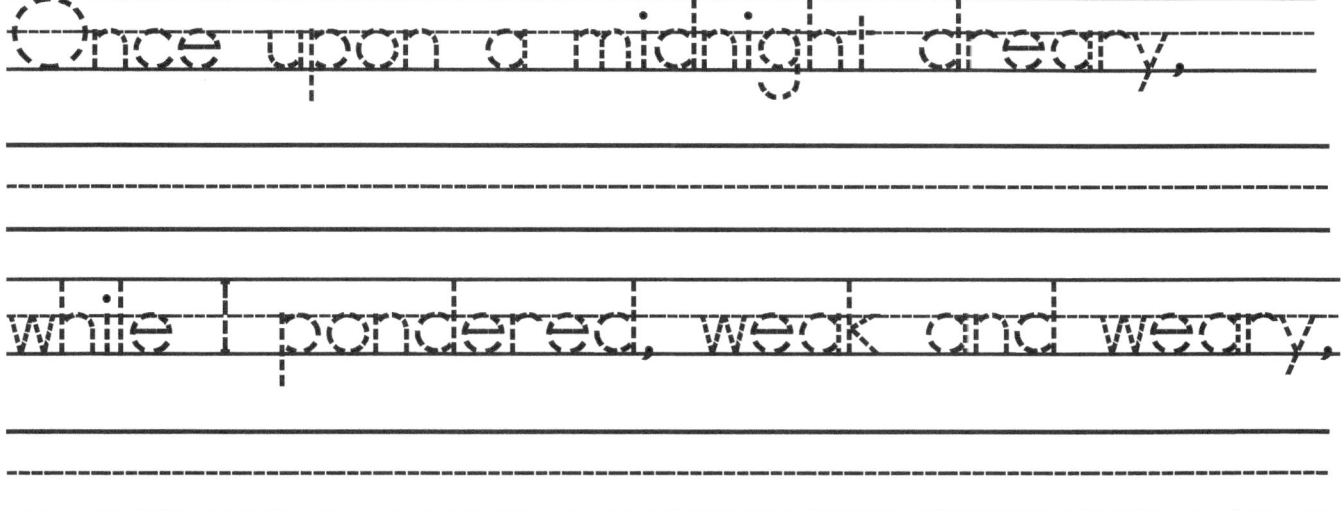

DRAW THE POEM (Sketch the frightened narrator hearing the raven rapping at the door with its beak.)

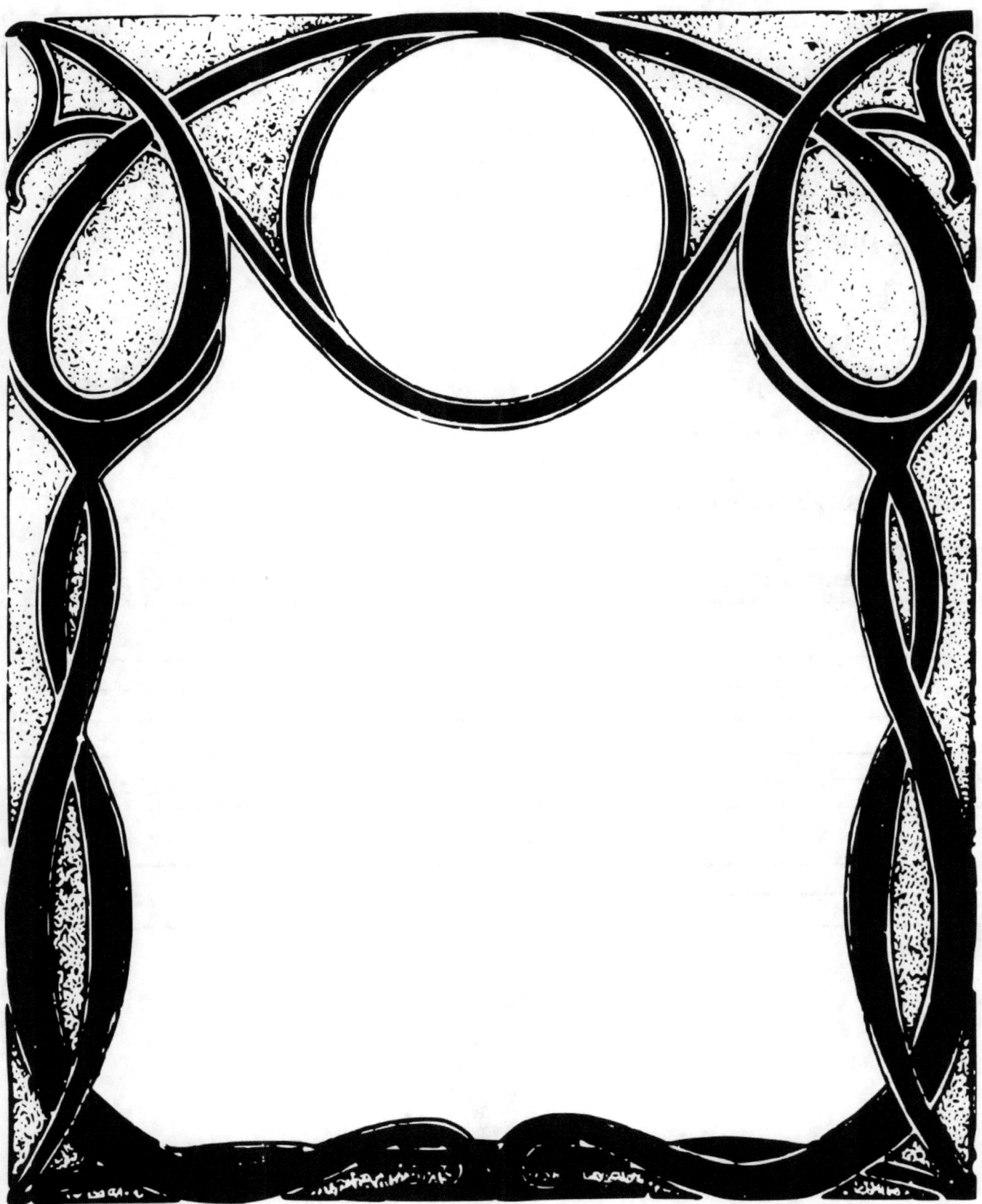

LESSON 35: "THE RAVEN" v. 7-12
BY EDGAR ALLAN POE

FEATURED POEM

7. Open here I flung the shutter, when, with many a flirt and flutter,

In there stepped a stately Raven, of the saintly days of yore;

Not the least obeisance made he, not a minute stopped or stayed he;

But with mien of lord or lady, perched above my chamber door-

Perched above a bust of Pallas, just above my chamber door-

Perched, and sat, and nothing more.

8. Then this ebony bird beguiling my sad fancy into smiling,

By the grave and stern decorum of the countenance it wore;

"Though thy crest be shorn and shaven, thou," I said, "art sure, no craven;

Ghastly, grim, and ancient Raven, wandering from the nightly shore,

Tell me what thy lordly name is on the night's Plutonian shore?"

Quoth the Raven, "Nevermore."

9. Much I marveled this ungainly fowl to hear discourse so plainly,

Though its answer, little meaning, little relevancy bore;

For we cannot help agreeing that no living human being

Ever yet was blessed with seeing bird above his chamber door-

Bird or beast upon the sculptured bust above his chamber door

With such a name as "Nevermore."

10. But the Raven, sitting lonely on that placid bust, spoke only

That one word, as if his soul in that one word he did outpour;

Nothing further then he uttered, not a feather then he fluttered,

Till I scarcely more than muttered-"Other friends have flown before,

On the morrow he will leave me, as my hopes have flown before."

Then the bird said, "Nevermore."

11. Startled by the stillness broken by reply so aptly spoken,

"Doubtless," said I, "what it utters is its only stock and store,

Caught from some unhappy master, whom unmerciful disaster

Followed fast and followed faster, till his songs one burden bore-

Till the dirges of his hope this melancholy burden bore-

Of 'Never, nevermore,'"

12. But the Raven still beguiling all my sad soul into smiling,

Straight I wheeled a cushioned seat in front of bird, and bust, and door;

Then upon the velvet sinking, I betook myself to linking

Fancy into fancy, thinking what this ominous bird of yore-

What this grim, ungainly, ghastly, gaunt, and ominous bird of yore

Meant in croaking "Nevermore."

SYNOPSIS

The narrator hears a tapping and throws open his shutter. A Raven enters and perches above a bust of Pallas Athena, Greek goddess of wisdom. At first the narrator feels relieved. The narrator asks the Raven his name, and the Raven answers, "Nevermore." The narrator states the Raven will leave tomorrow. The Raven sits on the bust and says "Nevermore" again. The narrator rationalizes that the bird learned the word from his prior master who suffered some disaster. The narrator sits and looks at the bird, trying to figure out some explanation for what is happening.

ENRICHMENT ACTIVITIES

1. **Recite Poem Information**
   Practice reciting the title of the poem and the name of the poet.
2. **Narrate the Poem**
   Verbally recount poem events in your own words.
3. **Study the Poem Pictures**
   Study the poem pictures and describe how they relate to the poem.
4. **Can You Find It?**
   - Find the following in the first poem picture:
     - The Poem Narrator
     - Shutters
     - Curtains
     - The Raven
     - Chair
     - Foot Rest
   - Find the following in the second poem picture:
     - The Raven
     - Pallas
     - Bust
     - Helmet
     - Door
5. **Explore Rhyming**
   Find and recite the rhyming words in the poem.

VOCABULARY

Students Recite Words	Students Listen to the Definitions
yore	Of long ago or former times.
obeisance	Showing respect.
mien	A person's look or manner.
bust	A sculpture of a person's head, shoulders, and chest.

Students Recite Words	Students Listen to the Definitions
Pallas	Pallas Athena, Greek goddess of wisdom.
beguiling	Charming or enchanting someone, sometimes in a deceptive way.
decorum	Behavior in keeping with good taste and propriety.
countenance	A person's face or facial expression.
plutonian	Of or associated with Pluto, Greek god of the underworld.
aptly	Appropriate or suitable in the circumstances.
dirge	A lament for the dead, especially one forming part of a funeral rite.
betook	To go to, to cause to go.

REVIEW QUESTIONS

1. What is the title of the poem?
2. What happens in theses verses of the poem?
3. Where does the poem take place?
4. Who are the characters in the poem?

TRACEWORK AND/OR COPYWORK

DRAW THE POEM (Illustrate the Raven croaking "Nevermore.")

LESSON 36: "THE RAVEN" v. 13-18
BY EDGAR ALLAN POE

FEATURED POEM

13. Thus I sat engaged in guessing, but no syllable expressing

To the fowl whose fiery eyes now burned into my bosom's core;

This and more I sat divining, with my head at ease reclining

On the cushion's velvet lining, that the lamp-light gloated o'er,

But whose velvet violet lining, with the lamp-light gloating o'er,

She shall press, ah, nevermore!

14. Then methought the air grew denser, perfumed from an unseen censer

Swung by seraphim, whose footfalls twinkled on the tufted floor.

"Wretch," I cried, "thy God hath lent thee-by these angels He hath sent thee

Respite-respite and nepenthe from my memories of Lenore!

Quaff, oh, quaff this kind nepenthe, and forget this lost Lenore!"

Quoth the Raven, "Nevermore."

15. "Prophet," said I, "thing of evil-prophet still, if bird or devil!

Whether tempter sent, or whether tempest tossed thee here ashore

Desolate, yet all undaunted, on this desert land enchanted,

On this home by horror haunted-tell me truly, I implore,

Is there-is there balm in Gilead?-tell me, tell me, I implore!"

Quoth the Raven, "Nevermore."

16. "Prophet," said I, "thing of evil!-prophet still if bird or devil!

By that heaven that bends above us-by that God we both adore-

Tell this soul, with sorrow laden, if, within the distant Aidenn

It shall clasp a sainted maiden, whom the angels name Lenore!

Clasp a rare and radiant maiden, whom the angels name Lenore?"

Quoth the Raven, "Nevermore."

17. "Be that our sign of parting, bird or fiend," I shrieked, upstarting-

"Get thee back into the tempest and the night's Plutonian shore;

Leave no black plume as a token of that lie thy soul hath spoken,

Leave my loneliness unbroken-quit the bust above my door,

Take thy beak from out my heart and take thy form from off my door!"

Quoth the Raven, "Nevermore."

18. And the Raven, never flitting, still is sitting, still is sitting,

On the pallid bust of Pallas, just above my chamber door;

And his eyes have all the seeming of a demon's that is dreaming,

And the lamp-light o'er him streaming, throws his shadow on the floor;

And my soul from out that shadow, that lies floating on the floor,

Shall be lifted-nevermore!

SYNOPSIS

The Raven's eyes burn through the narrator. The narrator smells incense and believes he hears angels nearby. The narrator calls the Raven a wretch and wishes for a potion to forget Lenore. The Raven just croaks back, "Nevermore." The narrator wonders whether evil sent the Raven or the Raven was sent to soothe him. The raven croaks again, "Nevermore." The narrator asks whether his soul will be reunited with Lenore in heaven. The Raven says again, "Nevermore." The narrator demands the Raven go back to where it came from, but the Raven only replies, "Nevermore." The Raven does not leave, sitting and casting a shadow of sadness over the narrator that shall be lifted nevermore.

ENRICHMENT ACTIVITIES

1. **Recite Poem Information**
   Practice reciting the title of the poem and the name of the poet.

2. **Narrate the Poem**
   Verbally recount poem events in your own words.

3. **Study the Poem Pictures**
   Study the poem pictures and describe how they relate to the poem.

4. **Can You Find It?**
   - Find the following in the first poem picture:
     - The Raven
     - Pallas
     - Bust
     - Door
     - Seraphim
     - The Narrator
     - Chair
   - Find the following in the second poem picture:
     - The Raven
     - Pallas
     - Bust
     - Door
     - Hanging Pictures
     - The Narrator
     - Chair
     - Shadow

5. **Explore Rhyming**
   Find and recite the rhyming words in the poem.

VOCABULARY

Students Recite Words	Students Listen to the Definitions
divining	Discover something by guesswork, intuition, or supernatural insight.
censer	A container in which incense is burned.
incense	A gum, spice, or other substance that is burned for the sweet smell it produces.
seraphim	Angel.
nepenthe	A drug described in Homer's Odyssey as banishing grief or trouble from a person's mind.
quaff	To drink heartily.
tempest	A violent windy storm.
balm	A fragrant ointment or preparation used to heal or soothe the skin.
Gilead	A region in modern-day Jordan. In the poem, is a reference to a Biblical quote, "Is there no balm in Gilead?" meaning is there no peace, no end to the pain and suffering?
Aidenn	Paradise or heaven.
fiend	A wicked or cruel person.
pallid	Pale.

REVIEW QUESTIONS

1. What is the title of the poem?
2. What happens in the poem?
3. Where does the poem take place?
4. Who are the characters in the poem?

TRACEWORK AND/OR COPYWORK

My soul from out that shadow,

that lies floating on the floor,

Shall be lifted-nevermore!

DRAW THE POEM (Create a spooky representation of the raven haunting the poem narrator.)

ELEMENTARY POETRY VOLUME 2: POETRY OF FABLES, FAIRIES, AND FAUNA

ANSWERS TO REVIEW QUESTIONS

LESSON 1
1. **What is the title of the poem?** The title of the poem is "The Frog Who Wished to be as Big as the Ox."
2. **What happens in the poem?** A little frog tries to be something he is not and suffers the consequences.
3. **What is the setting of the poem?** The poem takes place outdoors in a bog.
4. **Who are the characters in the poem?** The characters include a little frog, his sister, and an ox.
5. **What does the poem teach the reader?** The poem teaches us there are certain things about ourselves which we cannot change.

LESSON 2
1. **What is the title of the poem?** The title of the poem is "The Grasshopper and the Ant."
2. **What happens in the poem?** An ant works hard all summer storing food for the long, cold winter while a grasshopper does little to prepare and sings the summer days away. During winter, the grasshopper runs out of food and the ant tells him to go dance for his supper.
3. **What is the setting of the poem?** The poem takes place mostly in the homes of the Grasshopper and the Ant.
4. **Who are the characters in the poem?** The characters are the grasshopper and the ant.
5. **What does the poem teach the reader?** To work hard and save for the tough times. You may only be able to rely upon yourself.

LESSON 3
1. **What is the title of the poem?** The title of the poem is "The Cat and the Fox."
2. **What happens in the poem?** A fox brags to a cat about knowing many tricks. When dogs chase the cat and the fox, the cat's one trick of climbing a tree saves the cat, while the fox perishes despite knowing many tricks.
3. **What is the setting of the poem?** The poem takes place outdoors.
4. **Who are the characters in the poem?** The characters are the cat, the fox, and the dogs.
5. **What does the poem teach the reader?** The poem teaches us that knowing the right trick for a situation is far more important than the number of tricks someone knows.

LESSON 4
1. **What is the title of the poem?** The title of the poem is "The Dog and His Image."
2. **What happens in the poem?** A greedy dog tries to steal his reflection's bone, losing his bone in the process.
3. **What is the setting of the poem?** The poem takes place outdoors, next to a stream.
4. **Who are the characters in the poem?** The characters are the dog and his reflection.
5. **What does the poem teach the reader?** The poem teaches us to be grateful for what we have. It also reminds us not to be greedy or we may lose what we already have.

LESSON 5
1. **What is the title of the poem?** The title of the poem is "The Raven and the Fox."
2. **What happens in the poem?** A fox falsely flatters a raven into dropping a tasty morsel, which the fox gobbles up.
3. **What is the setting of the poem?** The poem takes place outdoors, in and under a tree.
4. **Who are the characters in the poem?** The characters are the raven and the fox.
5. **What does the poem teach the reader?** The poem teaches us to be wary of false flattery. It also suggests we know your own strengths and weaknesses.

LESSON 6
1. **What is the title of the poem?** The title of the poem is "The City Mouse and the Country Mouse."
2. **What happens in the poem?** A country mouse enjoys the food but not the dangers and uncertainties of the city.

3. **What is the setting of the poem?** The poem takes place in a city house.
4. **Who are the characters in the poem?** The characters are the city mouse and the country mouse.
5. **What does the poem teach the reader?** The poem teaches us that for some, peace of mind trumps fancy food and luxuries.

LESSON 7
1. **What is the title of the poem?** The title of the poem is "The Dove and the Ant."
2. **What happens in the poem?** A dove saves an ant. Later, the ant returns the favor.
3. **Where does the poem take place?** The poem takes place outside, near a brook.
4. **Who are the characters in the poem?** The characters are the dove, and ant, and the man.
5. **What does the poem teach the reader?** The poem teaches us that if we help others and we may be helped in return.

LESSON 8
1. **What is the title of the poem?** The title of the poem is "The Fox and the Grapes."
2. **What happens in the poem?** A fox claims a bunch of grapes are sour because he can't have them.
3. **Where does the poem take place?** The poem takes place outside, near some grape vines.
4. **Who are the characters in the poem?** The sole character is the fox.
5. **What does the poem teach the reader?** To poem points out that people sometimes lie to themselves to cope with failure.

LESSON 9
1. **What is the title of the poem?** The title of the poem is "The Fox and the Stork."
2. **What happens in the poem?** A fox is a poor dinner host to a stork and the stork returns the favor.
3. **Where does the poem take place?** The poem takes place at the fox's home and the stork's home.
4. **Who are the characters in the poem?** The characters are a fox and a stork.
5. **What does the poem teach the reader?** The poem advises us to treat others as we want to be treated.

LESSON 10
1. **What is the title of the poem?** The title of the poem is "The Hare and the Tortoise."
2. **What happens in the poem?** A slow tortoise wins a race with a much faster hare.
3. **Where does the poem take place?** The poem takes place outside.
4. **Who are the characters in the poem?** The characters are a hare and a tortoise.
5. **What does the poem teach the reader?** The poem teaches us that slow and steady wins the race.

LESSON 11
1. **What is the title of the poem?** The title of the poem is "The Heron Who Was Hard to Please."
2. **What happens in the poem?** A haughty stork ignores a bounty of fish, waiting for something better, and ends up with just a snail for dinner.
3. **Where does the poem take place?** The poem takes place on the banks of a creek.
4. **Who are the characters in the poem?** A characters include a stork, some fish, and a snail.
5. **What does the poem teach the reader?** The poem teaches us to value our current opportunities. Something better may never come along.

LESSON 12
1. **What is the title of the poem?** The title of the poem is "The Lion and the Gnat."
2. **What happens in the poem?** An arrogant gnat torments an arrogant lion, then is eaten by a spider.
3. **Where does the poem take place?** The poem takes place outside.
4. **Who are the characters in the poem?** The characters include the lion, the gnat, and the spider.
5. **What does the poem teach the reader?** The poem teaches us that arrogance is always misplaced. No matter how smart, fast, strong, etc. you are, don't be overconfident. Realize everyone is fallible.

LESSON 13
1. **What is the title of the poem?** The title of the poem is "The Fairies."
2. **What happens in the poem?** A group of fairies and their king and queen scare hunters, plant trees, steal children, and get revenge.
3. **Where does the poem take place?** The poem takes place on a mountain and in a glen in Ireland.
4. **Who are the characters in the poem?** Characters include the fairies, the narrator, little Bridget, and hunters.
5. **What does the poem teach the reader?** The poem invites the reader to ponder how the wee folk might live.

LESSON 14
1. **What is the title of the poem?** The title of the poem is "The Elf Singing."
2. **What happens in the poem?** A snake tries to eat a fairy but ends up being eaten by a mole.
3. **Where does the poem take place?** The poem takes place outside on a tree.
4. **Who are the characters in the poem?** Characters include the elf, the snake, and the mole.
5. **What does the poem teach the reader?** In some circumstances, singing can both uplift us and save us. Sometimes predators become prey.

LESSON 15
1. **What is the title of the poem?** The title of the poem is "The Fairy King."
2. **What happens in the poem?** A queen steals an old king's crown and wears it. Thus, she disappears and the king grows young.
3. **Where does the poem take place?** Where the poem takes place is unclear, but perhaps "high on the hilltop."
4. **Who are the characters in the poem?** Characters include the old Fairy King and the Witch of the Wold.
5. **What does the poem teach the reader?** Stealing things from others may lead to unanticipated consequences.

LESSON 16
1. **What is the title of the poem?** The title of the poem is "Chorus of Fairies."
2. **What happens in the poem?** The poem describes the fun and work on a beautiful summer day.
3. **Where does the poem take place?** The poem takes place in flowery meadows and forest shadows.
4. **Who are the characters in the poem?** Characters include the narrator of the poem and their companions.
5. **What does the poem teach the reader?** The poem reminds the reader to cherish the beauty of a summer day and to whistle while they work.

LESSON 17
1. **What is the title of the poem?** The title of the poem is "The Leprechaun or the Fairy Shoemaker."
2. **Where does the poem take place?** The poem takes place mainly up on the mound in the castle-ditch.
3. **What happens in the poem?** The narrator asks us whether we have heard the hammer of the Elfin shoemaker working up on the mound. The narrator advises if you capture the shoemaker you may use him to make yourself rich. The narrator saw him once, but before he could capture him the shoemaker disappeared.
4. **Who are the characters in the poem?** Characters include the narrator and the shoemaker.

LESSON 18
1. **What is the title of the poem?** The title of the poem is "Robin Redbreast."
2. **What happens in the poem?** The poem warns a robin that winter is near and describes the changes of the fall season.
3. **Who are the characters in the poem?** Characters include the narrator, the robin, other fauna.
4. **What does the poem teach the reader?** The poem reminds us to prepare for upcoming winters.

LESSON 19
1. **What is the title of the poem?** The title of the poem is "Dreaming."
2. **What happens in the poem?** A dream slips down from the sky to be experienced by a little boy named Fred.
3. **Where does the poem take place?** The poem takes place in the bedroom of little Fred and inside his

imagination.
4. **Who are the characters in the poem?** Characters include the narrator and little Fred.
5. **What does the poem teach the reader?** The poem sparks the reader's imagination.

LESSON 20
1. **What is the title of the poem?** The title of the poem is "I Love You, Dear."
2. **What happens in the poem?** The narrator expresses their adoration for another.
3. **Who are the characters in the poem?** Characters include the narrator and their "dear."
4. **What does the poem teach the reader?** The poem's expression of love reminds us of our own beloved "dears."

LESSON 21
1. **What is the title of the poem?** The title of the poem is "Seasons."
2. **What happens in the poem?** The narrator discusses the unique benefits of each of the four seasons.
3. **Who are the characters in the poem?** The character is the narrator.
4. **What does the poem teach the reader?** The poem reminds the reader of the delights of each of the seasons.

LESSON 22
1. **What is the title of the poem?** The title of the poem is "The Cat and the Dog."
2. **What happens in the poem?** A cat and dog race to see who can stay inside, and a beggar strikes the dog with his staff, causing the dog to lose. Dogs bark at beggars since then.
3. **Who are the characters in the poem?** Characters include the man, cat, dog, and the beggar.
4. **What does the poem teach the reader?** The poem is a fable that seeks to explain why dogs bark at strangers/beggars and perhaps why dogs and cats do not get along.

LESSON 23
1. **What is the title of the poem?** The title of the poem is "The Bird."
2. **What happens in the poem?** A child tries to convince a bird to become her pet, but the bird refuses, preferring the freedom of living in the wild.
3. **Who are the characters in the poem?** Characters include the child and the bird.
4. **What does the poem teach the reader?** To many, freedom is more valuable than riches.

LESSON 24
1. **What is the title of the poem?** The title of the poem is "Wishing."
2. **What happens in the poem?** The narrator wishes to be a primrose, a tree, and a robin and thinks over the advantages and disadvantages.
3. **Who are the characters in the poem?** The character is the narrator.
4. **What does the poem teach the reader?** It is often best to just be yourself.

LESSON 25
1. **What is the title of the poem?** The title of the poem is "I Saw a Little Birdie Fly."
2. **Where does the poem take place?** The poem takes place outdoors.
3. **What happens in the poem?** The narrator asks a bird to whom it sings. The bird replies it sings to Amy. The bird asks for payment for its song, a crumb and a smile from Amy.
4. **Who are the characters in the poem?** Characters include the narrator, the birdie, and Amy.

LESSON 26
1. **What is the title of the poem?** The title of the poem is "A Mountain Round."
2. **Where does the poem take place?** The poem takes place in a meadow outdoors under the moonlight.
3. **What happens in the poem?** The narrator calls for their neighbors to dance to music under the moonlight.
4. **Who are the characters in the poem?** Characters include the narrator and their neighbors.

5. **What does the poem teach the reader?** Dancing under the moonlight can be exhilarating.

LESSON 27
1. **What is the title of the poem?** The title of the poem is "Birds' Names."
2. **What happens in the poem?** The poem describes the characteristics and appearance of various birds. When Mag steals the eggs from the other birds, they attack her and pluck her of all her feathers.
3. **Who are the characters in the poem?** The narrator and the many birds they describe.
4. **What does the Mag do that upsets the other birds?** Mag steals their eggs.
5. **How do the birds get revenge on Mag?** They pluck all her feathers off.

LESSON 28
1. **What is the title of the poem?** The title of the poem is "Nick Spence."
2. **What happens in the poem?** Nick Spence sold his master's cow for far too little money and didn't feel bad about it, so the narrator recommends punishment.
3. **Where does the poem take place?** The poem takes place on a farm in a rural area.
4. **Who are the characters in the poem?** Characters include Nick Spence, Nick's Master, and Johnny.
5. **What does the poem teach the reader?** The poem teaches the reader to be wise in our actions or to suffer the consequences.

LESSON 29
1. **What is the title of the poem?** The title of the poem is "Riding."
2. **What happens in the poem?** A lady and lord riding horseback encounter a poor man riding a donkey. The lord angrily orders the poor man out of their way, and the man refuses. The lady treats the poor man kindly, and he moves off to the side.
3. **Who are the characters in the poem?** Characters include a lady, a lord, and a cadger.
4. **What does the poem teach the reader?** Treat others as you would like to be treated yourself.

LESSON 30
1. **What is the title of the poem?** The title of the poem is "Tom Cricket."
2. **What happens in the poem?** Tom Cricket plays for some dancing Cockroaches until they refuse to bring him some food. When he stops playing, the Cockroaches want revenge, but the Cook and the Scullion interrupt their plot.
3. **Who are the characters in the poem?** Characters include Tom Cricket, cockroaches, the cook and scullery.
4. **What does the poem teach the reader?** People may be ungrateful even if you do them a favor.

LESSON 31
1. **What is the title of the poem?** The title of the poem is "Let Dogs Delight to Bark and Bite."
2. **What happens in the poem?** The narrators remarks that although dogs bark and bite and bears and lions growl and fight, children are not meant to do the same.
3. **Who are the characters in the poem?** Characters include the narrator, the audience (children), dogs, bears, and lions.
4. **What does the poem teach the reader?** The poem advises children they were not meant to bite and fight like animals.

LESSON 32
1. **What is the title of the poem?** The title of the poem is "The Owl and the Pussy-Cat."
2. **What happens in the poem?** The Owl and the Pussy-Cat sail on the sea, buy a ring from a piggy, get married, and dance in the light of the moon.
3. **Where does the poem take place?** The poem takes place on the sea.
4. **Who are the characters in the poem?** Characters include the owl, the pussy-cat, the piggy, and the turkey.

LESSON 33
1. **What is the title of the poem?** The title of the poem is "A Chrysalis."
2. **What happens in the poem?** Both a butterfly and a little girl shed their chrysalises.
3. **Where does the poem take place?** The poem takes place outdoors, perhaps in a garden.
4. **Who are the characters in the poem?** The narrator, Mädchen, and the butterfly.
5. **What does the poem teach the reader?** The poem explores the possibility that we become something wondrous after our deaths.

LESSON 34
1. **What is the title of the poem?** The title of the poem is "The Raven" (v. 1-6).
2. **What happens in these verses of the poem?** The narrator hears a tapping at his door. He feels nervous, but assumes himself it is no more than a visitor knocking. He hears a tapping at his door and opens the door, but no one is there. All he hears is a whisper of the word, "Lenore." He goes back into his chamber and the tapping at his door starts again, even louder. He tells himself it is only the wind.
3. **Where does the poem take place?** The poem takes place in the narrator's chamber.
4. **Who are the characters in the poem?** The characters are the narrator and the Raven.

LESSON 35
1. **What is the title of the poem?** The title of the poem is "The Raven" (v. 7-12).
2. **What happens in these verses of the poem?** The narrator hears a tapping and throws open his shutter. A Raven enters and perches above a bust of Pallas Athena, Greek goddess of wisdom. At first the narrator feels relieved. The narrator asks the Raven his name, and the Raven answers, "Nevermore." The bird sits on the bust and says "Nevermore" again. The narrator rationalizes that the bird learned the word from his prior master who suffered some disaster. The narrator sits and looks at the bird, trying to figure out some explanation for what is happening.
3. **Where does the poem take place?** The poem takes place in the narrator's chamber.
4. **Who are the characters in the poem?** The characters are the narrator and the Raven.

LESSON 36
1. **What is the title of the poem?** The title of the poem is "The Raven" (v. 13-18).
2. **What happens in these verses of the poem?** The narrator smells incense and believes he hears angels nearby. He calls the Raven a wretch and wishes for a potion to make him forget Lenore. The narrator wonders whether evil sent the Raven or if the Raven has been sent to soothe him. The narrator asks the Raven whether his soul will be reunited with Lenore in heaven. The narrator demands the Raven go back to where it came from, but all the Raven will do is croak, "Nevermore." The Raven does not leave, sitting and casting a shadow of sadness over the narrator that shall be lifted nevermore.
3. **Where does the poem take place?** The poem takes place in the narrator's chamber.
4. **Who are the characters in the poem?** The characters are the narrator and the Raven.

REFERENCES AND ADDITIONAL READING

1. **Cover Image**
   a. Title: "Take the Fair Face of Woman, and Gently Suspending, With Butterflies, Flowers, and Jewels Attending, Thus Your Fairy is Made of Most Beautiful Things"
   b. Artist: Sophie Gengembre Anderson
   c. Original Source: commons.wikimedia.org/wiki/File:SophieAndersonTakethefairfaceofWoman.jpg
   d. License: The author died in 1903, so this work is in the public domain in its country of origin and other countries and areas where the copyright term is the author's life plus 100 years or less. This work is in the public domain in the United States because it was published (or registered with the U.S. Copyright Office) before January 1, 1925.
2. **Lessons 1-12: Poem Text and Illustrations**
   a. Larned, W.T. and Rae, John. "Fables in Rhyme for Little Folks From the French of La Fontaine" (1918, {PD-US})
   b. Source: http://www.gutenberg.org/files/24108/24108-h/24108-h.htm
   c. License: This work is in the public domain in the United States because it was published (or registered with the U.S. Copyright Office) before January 1, 1925.
3. **Lessons 1-12: Additional Poem Illustrations**
   a. Winter, Milo. "The Aesop for Children" (1919, {PD-US})
   b. Source: https://www.gutenberg.org/files/19994/19994-h/19994-h.htm#Page_88
   c. License: This work is in the public domain in the United States because it was published (or registered with the U.S. Copyright Office) before January 1, 1925.
4. **Lesson 13-30: Poem Text**
   a. Allingham, William. "Rhymes for the Young Folks" (1887, {PD-US})
   b. Source: http://www.gutenberg.org/files/46702/46702-h/46702-h.htm
   c. License: This work is in the public domain in the United States because it was published (or registered with the U.S. Copyright Office) before January 1, 1925
5. **Lessons 31-36: Poem Text**
   a. Burt, Mary E. "Poems Every Child Should Know" (1904, {PD-US})
   b. Source: https://www.gutenberg.org/files/16436/16436-h/16436-h.htm
   c. License: This work is in the public domain in the United States because it was published (or registered with the U.S. Copyright Office) before January 1, 1925.
6. **Lesson 32: "The Owl and the Pussycat" Illustrations**
   a. Poem Illustrations by Foster, William. "The Owl & the Pussy Cat and The Duck & the Kangaroo" (1889, {PD-US})
   b. Source: https://www.gutenberg.org/files/20113/20113-h/20113-h.htm
   c. License: This work is in the public domain in the United States because it was published (or registered with the U.S. Copyright Office) before January 1, 1925.
7. **Lessons 34-36: "The Raven" Illustrations**
   a. Poem Illustrations by Doré, Gustave. "The Raven" (1884, {PD-US})
   b. Source: https://www.gutenberg.org/files/17192/17192-h/17192-h.htm
   c. License: This work is in the public domain in the United States because it was published (or registered with the U.S. Copyright Office) before January 1, 1925.
8. ***All Other Clipart and Images. Open Clipart. openclipart.org. n.p. ({PD-US})***
9. ***All Definitions. Wiktionary: Public Domain Sources. en.wiktionary.org. n.p. ({PD-US}).***

ABOUT THE AUTHOR

Sonja Glumich is a scientist, educator, wife, and mother who is inspired by Charlotte Mason's living works approach to homeschooling. She is the founder of Under the Home (underthehome.org), an online homeschool curriculum featuring free courses in art history, poetry, prose, music, history, science, studio art, mathematics, reading, and Shakespeare. Sonja's husband, Chris, homeschools their three school-aged children using the Under the Home curriculum as featured in this book.

Sonja graduated magna cum laude with bachelor's degrees in biology, chemistry, and computer science and later earned a master's degree in information technology. She has also completed education classes and student teaching leading to certification to teach secondary science.

Sonja has experience teaching students of all ages, from preschool to graduate school, including as a middle school and high school science public school teacher. She has also served as an Adjunct Professor for Syracuse University and co-created two graduate-level cyber courses. She currently works as a computer scientist for the Air Force Research Laboratory. Her current research and education interests are security systems engineering, cyber vulnerability assessments, and everything homeschooling.